Welfare State
and
Welfare Society

Welfare State
and
Welfare Society

Illusion and Reality

by

WILLIAM A. ROBSON

Professor Emeritus of Public Administration in the University of London
Honorary Fellow and Lecturer at the London School of Economics

London
George Allen & Unwin Ltd
Ruskin House   Museum Street

First published in 1976

© George Allen & Unwin Ltd. 1976

ISBN 0 04 360040 9 hardback
0 04 360041 7 paperback

Printed in Great Britain
in 10 point Times Roman Type
by The Devonshire Press Ltd.
Barton Road, Torquay

Preface

I had three main aims in writing this book. First, to describe the sources and origins of the welfare state and to explain its nature. In doing so I have gathered together many different aspects of social life which have not hitherto been recognised as elements of the welfare state, but which I regard as forming an essential part of it. At the same time, I have shown how unsatisfactory is the view that the welfare state is mainly or exclusively concerned with providing social services of various kinds to the needy and under-privileged members of the community. It is my firm conviction that a welfare state worthy of the name must be concerned with the well-being of the entire nation.

A second aim has been to distinguish the welfare state from the welfare society. The welfare state is what Parliament has decreed and the Government does. The welfare society is what people do, feel and think about matters which bear on the general welfare. Failure to understand the difference is the cause of much conflict, friction and frustration, for there is often a yawning gulf between public policy and social attitudes. Unless people generally reflect the policies and assumptions of the welfare state in their attitudes and actions, it is impossible to fulfil the objectives of the welfare state.

The third aim is to inquire how far the hopes and expectations which were centred in the welfare state during the post-war years have been realised. To deal with this question in detail would require a work of much greater magnitude; but I have attempted to give a brief appraisal of some major features.

In the course of discussion I have indicated the economic, social and political policies which are likely to promote the purposes of a welfare state and also, *per contra*, the policies or doctrines which do not appear to be appropriate though they are often advocated in the name of the welfare state.

There is at present no philosophy of the welfare state and there is an urgent and deep need for such a theory. I cannot claim to have formulated a welfare state philosophy, but I have presented a number of propositions on which such a philosophy could be based. I find it strange that political philosophers should spend their time endlessly working over the texts of Hobbes, Locke, Rousseau, Mill and the other great men of the past, without attempting to bring the world of thought into relation with the contemporary world of action.

The short length of this book made it necessary to touch briefly on many matters which could and should be explored at much greater length. Many detailed studies of particular aspects are needed, and some have already been published. But the book I wanted to write was one which took a broad look over a wide horizon, and this inevitably involves the acceptance of certain limitations. The first book I wrote was a long-forgotten study entitled *The Relation of Wealth to Welfare* published in 1925. During the ensuing half-century I have been more or less continually concerned with problems of human welfare.

My references to Japan in Chapter VI are based on three visits to that country in recent years. During two of these visits I was asked to advise the Governor of Tokyo Metropolitan Government about problems concerning the administration, organisation and planning of the capital city. I have also visited the other great cities of Japan, and, in addition, have had exceptional opportunities for becoming acquainted at first hand with the problems of New York City.

My thanks are due to the Rockefeller Foundation for a grant which enabled me to appoint Mr W. H. Hampton as Research Assistant some time ago. I am grateful to Professor David Donnison for reading the manuscript and giving me the benefit of his comments. I am also greatly indebted to Mrs Shirley Grinter and Mrs Barbara Sloane for their valuable help in typing the manuscript.

WILLIAM A. ROBSON
London School of Economics and Political Science

Contents

Chapter I

The Nature of the Welfare State

Since the end of the Second World War the statement has been made with increasing emphasis that Britain is a welfare state. The statement is generally accepted by the British people, but not much effort has been made to discover what is the nature of the welfare state. The object of this book is not only to analyse the nature of the welfare state and its problems, but also to consider the meaning of welfare and the characteristics of a welfare society. A welfare state and a welfare society are by no means synonymous. Indeed, some of our most serious difficulties are due to the fact that we are trying to be a welfare state without being a welfare society.

The ideas underlying the welfare state are derived from many different sources. From the French Revolution came notions of liberty, equality and fraternity. From the utilitarian philosophy of Bentham and his disciples came the idea of the greatest happiness of the greatest number. From Bismarck[1] and Beveridge came the concepts of social insurance and social security. From the Fabian Socialists came the principle of the public ownership of basic industries and essential services. From Tawney came a renewed emphasis on equality and a rejection of avarice as the mainspring of social activity. From John Maynard Keynes and the Minority Report of the Poor Law Commission came doctrines for controlling the trade cycle and avoiding mass unemployment. From the Webbs came proposals for abolishing the causes of poverty and cleaning up the base of society. Many other thinkers, from Leonard Hobhouse[2] to Richard Titmuss, have contributed to the stream of ideas flowing into the concept of the welfare state. Above and beyond the specific contributions from these sources were the efforts to awaken the social conscience by writers like Dickens, Ruskin and William Morris; by social reformers like Lord Shaftesbury and Chadwick; by clerics such as Charles Kingsley, General Booth, Cardinal Manning and Canon Barnett; by economists such as John Stuart Mill and Henry George. There is, however, no positive or comprehensive philosophy, no ideology that underlies the many policies and programmes that are supposed to form part of the welfare state. This lack of a political or social philosophy is not peculiar to Britain. It exists equally in other countries which are generally regarded as welfare states, such as Sweden, New Zealand or India.[3]

Much thought has, however, been given to the evolution and the development of the welfare state. The history of successive stages has been traced in considerable detail;[4] and the late Richard Titmuss showed the successive impact of the South African War and the two World Wars on public opinion and government action in developing the personal health services.[5] In New Zealand, the initial impulse was humanitarian, though of a conservative rather than of a radical kind,[4] but the desire to relieve destitution was in course of time replaced by much wider and more positive aims.[6] The remark that 'welfare originally was a misnomer for the abolition of poverty, and social security was a misnomer for economic security' can be applied to other countries than New Zealand. In Sweden, welfare policy was originally directed to mitigating extreme need or suffering, but later became mainly concerned with the suppression of inequalities.[7]

Professor Marshall regards as the essential characteristics of the welfare state its intense individualism and its collectivism. The former confers on the individual an absolute right to receive welfare; the latter imposes a duty on the state to promote and safeguard the whole community, which may transcend the aggregation of individual claims.[8]

Several thinkers have devoted attention to the relations between the economic and the social aspects of the welfare state. Marshall considers that the welfare state has not rejected the capitalist market economy but gives it only qualified approval since there are some elements in civilised life of greater importance which can be attained only by restricting or supplanting the market. The result is 'a kind of capitalism softened by an injection of socialism, and many socialists disliked or mistrusted the mixture'.[9]

A somewhat similar view is taken by the Dutch writer Mr Piet Thoenes. The welfare state is in his view a new form of society which differs from the liberal state which preceded it and the socialist state which is its rival. It can also be distinguished from fascist and communist forms of social welfare, partly because of its democratic features and partly because it places less emphasis on collectivism.[10] The welfare state accepts a modified form of capitalism but retains the two basic elements of private property and the profit motive. He even asserts that welfare activities are a necessary condition for the survival of the capitalist system.[11] Like Marshall he sees it as a mixture of semi-socialism and semi-liberalism. To the advocates of those creeds it is inevitably a halfway house, 'to nobody is it a noble and inspiring ideal'.[12]

Mr Peter Shore, MP, writes of 'welfare capitalism' in a similar vein, but questions the kind of society we are creating. Is it, he asks, a welfare state or an opportunity state, a mixed economy or a post-capitalist society?[13] The answer is that it is all these things. Comment of this kind brings out the fact that the term welfare state does not designate a definite system. Hayek points out quite correctly that what goes under that name is a conglomeration of many diverse and even contradictory elements.[14] The late Karl Mannheim identified some of the contradictory philosophies that have a place in our social environment. Among them is the Christian ethic, based on the religion of love and universal brotherhood; beside it is the philosophy of the Enlightenment and liberalism, emphasising freedom and personal development, and commending wealth, security, happiness, tolerance and philanthropy as the means of achieving them. And finally comes the challenge of the socialists, with their doctrines of equality, social justice, security and a planned social order as the ultimate aims.[15]

There are, however, some socialists who present their faith from a very different point of view. Professor Norman Mackenzie, for example, is primarily concerned with avoiding oligarchy and defeating 'the faceless men of power' who control the economy. For him the central socialist objective is to secure control of the social and technical machinery which is now in the hands of an oligarchy. A second purpose is to make co-operation rather than conflict the essential motivation and thereby give to our lives a dignity and purpose they do not at present possess.[16] He calls our present polity the stalemate state, presumably because the struggle for power appeared (in 1958) to be in equilibrium. Instrumental socialism of this school, which is very much alive at the present time in Britain, has little relation to the objectives of the welfare state.

Instrumental socialism has played virtually no part in the social policies of contemporary Sweden. The Social Democratic Party, which has governed the country continuously since 1932 (except for three months in 1936), has introduced a great many welfare policies but has not replaced capitalism by a substantial amount of nationalised industry. The four traditions which have resulted in Swedish welfare policies are: (1) the humanitarian and Christian teaching which stresses the duty to help people in difficulty; (2) the patriarchal tradition, which imposed a considerable degree of authority on citizens who received help; (3) the philosophy of the Enlightenment and of English liberalism, which led to the concept of a national minimum, a safety net provided by the community as a protection against destitution; and (4) the democratic conviction that prosperity should be redistributed so as to eliminate pockets of poverty.[17] These traditions have not precluded a large concentration of wealth in the hands of a small minority of the nation.[18]

The position in Britain resembles in many respects that in Sweden, except that the public sector of the economy is much larger and the average income per head much smaller. The four aspirations underlying the welfare state in England have been identified as mutual aid, social welfare, social justice, and the reform of society without basic change.[19]

This raises the question of what constitutes basic change. If we are thinking of the economy, vast and profound changes have been introduced. Nationalisation of transport, coal, electricity and gas, the manufacture of steel, broadcasting, the national health service – these form a substantial proportion of the economy. Industrial training schemes, regional policies, control of the location of factories and offices, the regulation of demand, large-scale support for research and development intended to assist industry, control of wages and prices, high taxation, financial assistance to firms in difficulty, large subsidies to help build up a computer industry – policies such as these have resulted in a mixed and regulated economy which a mid-Victorian entrepreneur would scarcely recognise as capitalist. It is hardly open to question that a developed welfare state requires a controlled economy which will deal, or attempt to deal, with such matters as unemployment, inflation or deflation, the balance of payments, the level of investment, important sectors which are ailing, labour relations and many other matters.[20]

The welfare state is regarded by Thoenes as 'a form of society characterised by a system of democratic, government-sponsored welfare placed on a new footing and offering a guarantee of collective social care to its citizens, concurrently with the maintenance of a capitalist system of production'.[21] He then compares the welfare state with feudal, liberal and socialist societies, and contends that the expression is justified by the fact that it is the state which determines the form of the economic and social structure of society.

The use of the word 'state' is an acknowledgement of the active part played by the state in the social sphere.

Much of this analysis is questionable. A major theme of this book is that we are vainly trying to have a welfare state without having achieved a welfare society. In the second place, it is by no means clear that a capitalist system of production is essential to a welfare state; and in some respects it can be antithetic to it. It is equally clear that some socialist policies are antithetic to the welfare state. In any event Britain, like other Western countries, has a mixed and regulated economy with a substantial amount of public enterprise, price control, subsidisation of private firms, and other forms of intervention which have greatly modified the capitalist features of the economy.[22]

The tendency to regard society and the state as synonymous, and hence to consider the interests of the state as identical with those of society, is severely criticised by Professor Marsh. 'This identification is quite misleading', he writes, 'because the state is simply a form of organisation; the people organised politically to fulfil specified functions, to exercise a measure of (but not complete) control over relationships within society, and to act as a means of contact between states. Even in the most highly developed state there are forms of conduct, types of association, and informal relationships which have grown up within society and form part of its essential fabric over which the state has no control.'[23] Can anyone dispute the fact that much, if not most, private action and personal relationships are outside state control?

The question of what constitutes a welfare state can only be determined by agreement about its essential characteristics; and this is not a simple matter. Historically the welfare state in England originated in two separate spheres of action. One of them comprised the social services which Parliament initiated during the nineteenth century to deal with public health, education, factory conditions and housing. The other was the action taken in the twentieth century to relieve or to prevent destitution. This in time transformed the national attitude towards poverty, with far-reaching effects on public policy. The aims of these two streams of policy were initially negative: to prevent destitution and primary poverty; to prevent and cure disease; to protect employees against sweating, bad or unhealthy working conditions, and other forms of exploitation; to abolish slums and squalid living quarters; to eliminate ignorance and illiteracy; and to remove the grosser forms of inequality and privilege.[24] These negative purposes came to be generally accepted as necessary and desirable. The question of what positive aims should be pursued was, and is, a much more difficult problem to which I shall return in later chapters.

While many of the older evils which the welfare state was established to combat have disappeared or been greatly reduced in scope and magnitude, new evils have arisen of which we have become acutely aware in recent years, and with which the welfare state has not yet been able to cope effectively. They include the socially generated forms of disamenity or diswelfare such as urban blight, the pollution of the land, air, rivers and sea, higher levels of noise, the degradation of city life by motor vehicles, the holocaust of deaths and injuries on the roads, and such phenomena as premature retirement, hooliganism, drug addiction, the obsolescence of skills and redundancies.[25] Inflation has reached levels that threaten the security of the state and the stability of the nation.

What is not open to serious question is that a welfare state must be democratic. By that I mean the government must have been freely chosen by the citizens, who must be able to change it by peaceful means if they are dissatisfied with its performance. Moreover, public criticism of the government must be unrestricted and freely tolerated. Thoenes conceives of the welfare state solely or mainly in terms of its ability to provide material benefits, such as full employment, reasonable remuneration, purchasing power, social security, and cultural facilities, etc. He explicitly denies that the welfare state cannot exist except in a democracy.[26] But political and social freedom are in my opinion essential ingredients of the welfare state; and this excludes totalitarian regimes or dictatorships from being welfare states.[27]

Professor Alec Nove, an extremely fair-minded expert on Soviet affairs, has shown that the USSR has been making substantial and sustained progress in many spheres of social welfare, including health, education, leisure, greater equality of remuneration and social security. Among the motives for these improvements he mentions the doctrine that communism ensures abundance, the need of the party to appear to be improving the lot of the working masses, the desire to stimulate incentives to work, the need to guard against unfavourable comparisons arising from increasing foreign contacts, the communist belief in education, and the ever-present need to ensure political stability. No mention whatever is made in this analysis of welfare or the lack of it, of political freedom, of liberty of expression, of freedom to travel or to emigrate, of freedom to obtain or read foreign newspapers and books, of the terrible penalties imposed on critics of the regime or its policies. It is the absence of these essential goods of human well-being which makes one feel that Professor Nove has wrongly titled his essay 'Towards a Communist Welfare State'.[28]

The expression welfare state was unknown to Leonard Hobhouse, but some of his ideas are highly relevant to an understanding of its nature. He perceived liberalism and socialism as branches of a single humanitarian movement, and this latter is surely the basic force underlying the welfare state. The liberal, he wrote, stands for emancipation, and is the inheritor of a long tradition of those who have fought for liberty, who have struggled against government and its laws or against society because they crushed human development and repressed those who did not conform. In the face of this repression the liberal placed his faith in the unimpeded development of human abilities as the mainspring of progress. The socialist, he wrote, stands for the solidarity of society, for mutual responsibility and the duty of the strong to aid the weak. Co-operation and organisation are his watchwords. On this analysis the ideals of the liberal and the socialist were seen as complementary rather than conflicting.[29]

If those elements represent the quintessence of liberalism and socialism, it cannot be denied that the welfare state is the confluence where the two streams unite. But there are many aspects of the two creeds which are not included in Hobhouse's analysis and are not found in the welfare state.

What is more interesting, however, is to recall his warning that both the liberal and the socialist creed are easily perverted and are then in conflict.[30] The principle of liberty may be converted into an unlovely gospel of commercial competition, in which self-interest is sanctified as the supreme good and mutual help decried – a state of affairs (found among trade unions and their members nowadays as well as among their employers) in which merit is identified with success, and success measured by money-making ability. The collectivist approach is equally liable to suffer a process of distortion, whereby its liberal and democratic elements are gradually lost and bureaucratic organisation, centralisation, efficiency and expertise dominate the scene. Such distortion results in socialism losing its humane spirit. Gone are the protests against class tyranny, gone is its revolt against acquisitiveness and materialism, gone is its solicitude for the underdog, and in their place we have a concept of society as a mechanism controlled by wires radiating from a single centre. Humanity, liberty and justice are supplanted by the single word efficiency, and people are regarded as either experts or puppets.

Considerations such as these raise some profound questions

about what we mean by welfare. It is easy to say that a welfare state is one in which public policy is predominantly concerned with the welfare of its members; but this does not provide us with any insight into the nature of welfare. The examination of that question must be left for subsequent chapters.

NOTES

1 R. Mendelsohn, *Social Security in the British Commonwealth* (1954), p. 10.
2 For Hobhouse's contribution, see my Hobhouse Lecture, 'The Welfare State', *Hobhouse Memorial Lectures* (1957).
3 K. Gunnar Myrdal, *Beyond the Welfare State* (1960), p. 60.
4 M. Bruce, *The Coming of the Welfare State* (1961), p. ix.
5 Richard M. Titmuss, *Essays on the Welfare State* (1958), pp. 80–3.
6 J. B. Condliffe, *The Welfare State in New Zealand* (1959), p. 28; K. J. Scott (ed.), *Welfare in New Zealand* (1955), pp. 10–14.
7 G. Tegner, *Social Security in Sweden* (1956), p. 13.
8 T. H. Marshall, *Sociology at the Crossroads* (1963), p. 246.
9 ibid., p. 284.
10 Piet Thoenes, *The Elite in the Welfare State* (1966), p. 127.
11 ibid., p. 143.
12 ibid., p. 133.
13 Peter Shore, 'In the Room at the Top', in *Conviction*, ed. Norman Mackenzie (1958), p. 24.
14 F. A. Hayek, *The Constitution of Liberty* (1960), pp. 258–9.
15 Karl Mannheim, *Diagnosis of Our Time* (1943), p. 12.
16 Norman Mackenzie, 'After the Stalemate State', in *Conviction*, op. cit., p. 21.
17 Alva Myrdal, 'Report to the Swedish Social Democratic Party', *Towards Equality* (1971), pp. 88–9.
18 Larry Hufford, *Sweden: the Myth of Socialism*, Young Fabian Pamphlet 33 (1973), p. 1.
19 N. A. Smith, 'Theory and Practice of the Welfare State', *Political Quarterly*, Vol. 22 (1951), pp. 370–1.
20 Thoenes, op. cit., pp. 131–2.
21 ibid., p. 125.
22 For a fuller statement of the restrictions on free enterprise, see Myrdal, op cit., p. 61.
23 D. C. Marsh, *The Welfare State* (1970), p. 16.
24 See my Hobhouse Lecture, 'The Welfare State', published in *Hobhouse Memorial Lectures* (1957).
25 Richard M. Titmuss, *Commitment to Welfare* (1968), p. 133.
26 Thoenes, op. cit., pp. 130, 137. His view is that while democracy is a reasonable guarantee for the survival of a welfare state, the welfare state is no guarantee for the survival of democracy.
27 Professor Marsh shares my view on this question. See Marsh, op. cit., pp. 1–2.

28 *Problems of Communism,* No. 1, Vol. 9 (January–February 1960), pp. 1 et seq.
29 See my Hobhouse Lecture, op. cit., p. 6, quoting from his *Democracy and Reaction.*
30 L. T. Hobhouse, *Democracy and Reaction* (2nd revised edition, 1904), pp. 230–6.

Chapter II

Welfare State
Principles and Policies

As I pointed out in the previous chapter, a revolutionary change took place in the present century in the attitude towards poverty. For centuries poverty had been regarded as inevitable. It was generally assumed that the great majority of the people would be born poor and would remain poor, and a not inconsiderable proportion would become destitute. Individual cases of a deserving kind might be helped by almsgiving or charity; and men of exceptional ability and energy could climb into a higher level of society, but it was thought that little or nothing could be done to relieve poverty as a whole. The traditional view was questioned in Britain during the closing years of the nineteenth century. It was challenged with growing insistence in the twentieth century, when the spectacle of massive and widespread poverty in the midst of great wealth produced a sense of moral discomfort and intellectual misgivings among many of the leaders of public opinion. Social reformers, religious leaders and politicians could no longer accept the assumption that gross poverty and destitution were 'natural' and unavoidable, or ordained by providence. There was an awakening of the social conscience which gradually permeated all the political parties, and this led to a general demand for a national attack on the problem of poverty.[1]

The harshness and humiliation which had been deliberately introduced in 1834 had made the poor law, the only form of public aid for the destitute, hated and dreaded by the mass of the working class. Indeed, one of the objects of the 1834 legislation was to deter men and women from applying for relief. By the beginning of the twentieth century it was seen to be useless as a method of either curing or preventing destitution; and its principles were felt to be out of harmony with the newly awakened humanitarian spirit. The principles had, moreover, been to some extent undermined or abandoned by poor law guardians in various parts of the country.

Tentative steps in a new direction to protect the weakest and most vulnerable elements in society, such as the aged poor, the unemployed workman, the sweated worker, were taken by the Liberal Government of 1906–14, which introduced old-age pensions, health and unemployment insurance, minimum wage boards, and other measures on a strictly limited scale. From these modest beginnings the principle emerged that the state should eliminate the worst causes of poverty by fixing minimum standards of subsistence, medical care, education, housing, and nutrition by means of the social services, minimum wage legislation, social insurance and government regulation. These minimum standards were established to provide a floor below which it was assumed no one would be allowed to sink. The minimum standards were progressively raised as resources increased and confidence grew in the new methods.

The fullest development of the concept was made by Sidney Webb in a presidential address to the Social and Political Education League in 1908 on the subject of what he called 'the necessary basis of society'. This involved a national minimum standard of life imposed by the government in four main spheres of state action. These were: (1) The terms and conditions of employment, including a minimum rate of wages. (2) Leisure and recreation. Adequate time must be assured by law to every wage-earner for sleep, recreation, exercise of body or mind, the duties of citizenship and family life. (3) Health. This involved on the one hand a sanitary environment secured by a pure water supply, drainage and so forth, and on the other, medical services, hospitals and skilled nursing for the sick. (4) Education. There must be schools and colleges of every grade, and an adequate system of scholarships providing maintenance and tuition up to the postgraduate level for every scholar fitted to receive it. Only by some such policy, declared Sidney Webb, will modern industrial communities escape degeneration and decay. He claimed that his conception of the necessary basis of society did not imply an individualist or collectivist economic order. It was an indispensable foundation for every type of modern society or state, a basis on which any type of superstructure could be placed. He was careful to add that enforcing the national minimum 'will not interfere with the pecuniary profits or the power or the personal development of the exceptional man. The illimitable realm of the upward remains, without restriction, open to him . . . By fencing off the downward way, we divert the forces of competition along the upward way.'[2]

This statement made by Sidney Webb is remarkable for its prescience and generality. The only obvious omissions are the obligations of the state in regard to housing and full employment. But, considering the date when it was written, it is remarkably comprehensive, and its prescripts have been substantially fulfilled in almost every industrialised country.

Mrs Webb wrote nearly twenty-five years later that she thought they were sincere in asserting or implying that these conditions could be obtained without fundamentally changing the economic system, without sweeping away the landlords and the capitalists and penalising the profit-making motive. 'How otherwise', she asked, 'should we have sought the support of Conservative and Liberal leaders and of the majority of the working class who certainly were not at that time convinced Socialists?'[3]

The principle of a national minimum standard of life looks very different today from what it did when it was first formulated in legislation and public policy. It was originally conceived as an attempt to remedy poverty and prevent destitution. Nowadays we have become increasingly aware of the diverse needs of people needing help of a non-financial or partly non-financial kind. There are the handicapped and deprived children, the blind and the deaf, the one-parent families, the unmarried mothers, the drug addicts, the pregnant schoolgirls, the drop-outs from school and college, the homeless, the discharged prisoners vainly seeking work, the old man or woman living alone, the subnormal and severely subnormal children, the mentally ill discharged from hospital, the deserted wives without support, the alcoholics, the problem families, the newly arrived immigrants – one could continue the list.[4] No one who is at all familiar with even some of the problems facing these groups would assert that we have established a national minimum standard below which no one can fall. Nonetheless the position is immensely improved in comparison with what it was half a century ago.

Even more striking is the changed attitude concerning the role of the social services and the functions they perform. Before the Second World War the social services catered mainly for the working class and this was regarded as their proper scope. Sickness and unemployment insurance, and both contributory and non-contributory pensions were limited to employed persons whose incomes were well below the middle-class level. Primary education was free and secondary education available without charge only to those with low incomes subject to a means test. The basic aim was to abolish want and the method of financing provided a redistributive element. The redistribution was not only between the better-off and the worse-off income groups, but also through time, in that a worker received less income during his years of good health and employment, and more than he otherwise would when he was sick or old or unemployed.

After the Second World War the social services were extended to embrace the entire nation. This applied to the National Health Service, the national insurance schemes and secondary education. The abolition of want ceased to be the dominant motive. An unforeseen result was that the provision of free social services to the middle classes now appeared to some observers to have eliminated the redistributive element between rich and poor. As one academic pointed out, we cannot measure accurately the flow of incomes within and between groups; but our social services are not 'just gifts in the sack of the state Santa Claus which are distributed to the needy'.[5] Others declared that the main beneficiaries were now the middle classes.[6]

Some thinkers, both at home and abroad, were looking at the matter in quite different terms. In New Zealand the network of social services associated with the welfare state, originally conceived on humanitarian grounds to help the unfortunate, was now regarded as providing an assurance of a steady and expanding market for the products of industry, a form of insurance against industrial failure.[7]

In Sweden the Alva Myrdal Committee of the Social Democratic Party considered social policy as serving three separate functions. These were: (1) Social investment in the future, by means of preventive medicine, rehabilitation, and the care and education of children. (2) Income supplementation by means of pensions, housing allowances, subsidised medicine, etc. This is part of demand management. (3) Compensation to the victims of misfortune. These include the unemployed, those suffering industrial or highway accidents, and the physically or mentally handicapped. These policies taken together represent a continuous effort to create greater equality and increased security for the majority of the nation.[8] Professor Gunnar Myrdal added his own analysis of social reforms by pointing out that they had become increasingly directed to the welfare of the family and children; and that in the most advanced welfare states stress is laid on the socialisation of consumption as distinct from the old socialist proposals for the socialisation of large-scale industry and high finance.[9] Nearly twenty years earlier another Swedish writer had remarked that social policy in Sweden aimed at giving everyone in general, and the families with children in particular, a higher standard of living.[10]

Richard Titmuss, in one of his earlier essays, viewed all collectively provided services as designed to meet socially recognised needs, as manifestations of society's will to survive as an organic whole, and to assist the survival of some people who would go under if left unaided. Needs could therefore be thought of as both individual and social, as interrelated elements essential for the continued existence of the parts and the whole of society.[11] In a later analysis he identified in much greater detail the more important aims that underlie the social security system and the social service programmes. These comprise: (1) raising productivity per head, increasing the mobility of workers, and fostering economic growth; (2) safeguarding workers against industrial hazards, and sometimes discriminating in favour of those in the hardest and most dangerous occupations; (3) increasing or decreasing the birthrate; (4) preventing juvenile delinquency, crime and other forms of antisocial behaviour; (5) preventing sickness and ill health in order to increase productivity and the avoidance of suffering; (6) integrating everyone into society to enhance the sense of community and participation, to prevent alienation, and especially to integrate members of minority or ethnic groups and regional cultures; (7) increasing or diminishing inequalities of income and command over resources.[12] This complex conception is a far cry from the simple view of the social services as a means of imposing a national minimum standard of life. It is not surprising that Titmuss became increasingly aware of the difficulty of defining a social service in a satisfactory manner in view of the fact that many functions which are not officially included in that category have similar objectives. Thus, while approved schools and remand homes rank as social services, the probation service does not.[13] As the scope of state-provided services widen – to include, for example, in Sweden, government loans for furniture and equipment to newly married couples[14] or holidays for housewives – it becomes increasingly difficult to go beyond the statement that the social services are characterised by a direct concern with the personal well-being of individuals, and that any form of state intervention which satisfies this criterion is a social service.[15]

With the extension in the scope of the social services to include the middle classes, the redistribution element tended to diminish. The low income group was shown to be paying for its social service benefits in Findley Weaver's study in 1950;[16] yet two years later Iain MacLeod and Enoch Powell stated unequivocally that redistribution is a characteristic of the social services.[17] Professor Hayek asserted in 1960 that though a redistribution of incomes was never the avowed initial purpose of the apparatus of social security, it had become the actual and admitted aim everywhere.[18] He did not oppose the provision of a minimum level of welfare for all as incompatible with a free society. It was the sharing out of income on the basis of a concept of social justice which in his view cannot be reconciled with a free society.[19]

The policy of extending the social services to cover the entire nation came from the Labour Party although it may have led in some spheres to the middle classes benefiting to a greater extent than the working class. The motive which dictated the attitude of the Labour Party was that of removing any trace of inferiority falling on those who used the services, to eliminate the 'charity' element which still persisted among those who regarded what they called 'the dole' as equivalent to an act of philanthropy on the part of the state.[20]

The Labour Party's demand for universality was prompted by a strong desire to get away from the means test, which had for long been associated with the hated poor law. The response of Conservative politicians and those who share their views was to insist that if everyone is to be permitted to partake of social benefits, the available resources will be spread so thinly that genuine needs cannot be adequately met. Lady Wootton expressed a strongly held but unrealistic view by stating that 'the strongest argument for showering benefits upon rich and poor alike is that nobody need know who is poor and who is not'.[21] She added that this argument was based on egalitarian premises and was not valid unless all classes not only can, but do, use the same services. It is obvious, however, that the use of common services will not prevent people knowing who is rich and who is poor.

At the other extreme were those who argued that if services are intended to be based on need, it is wholly irrational to object to a means test in order to discover who are the needy.[22] Some Conservative politicians claimed that non-contributory benefits without an associated means test are an exception to the rule which can be explained only on historical grounds.[23] While publicists of this school based their arguments on the need to prevent the waste of resources on the better-off in order to provide more for those suffering hardship, part of the discussion rested on grounds of social psychology. Thus Richard Titmuss suggested that if all services are provided on a means-tested basis it would inculcate a sense of personal failure in the recipients and stigmatise them as a burden on society. The object of eligibility tests has always been to prevent and deter the unqualified from receiving benefits rather than to encourage the qualified. Moreover, selective services provided for the poor have always been of low quality.[24]

The importance of the psychological argument as an influence in the acceptability of a social service had been demonstrated earlier in the century with the advent of the national insurance scheme in 1911. From that time onwards the mythology about social insurance, the belief that every benefit had been paid for by those entitled to receive it, the conviction that rights had been created in place of charity, enabled the sick or unemployed workman to retain his self-respect as a contributor and as a recipient of benefits: such beliefs had become invested with a magical force which no analysis could dispel.[25]

A closer examination of the benefits in cash and in kind has shown the superficiality of many of the assumptions made both by the universalists and by those favouring selectivity. In a penetrating essay on the subject, Mr Mike Reddin explained why the debate on universal versus selective benefits cannot be a discussion of absolutes or diametrically opposed systems, but is concerned rather with the extension or curtailment of selective *vis-à-vis* universal benefits. He drew attention to the fact that while a service may be universally available, its use may be severely restricted as between groups, and that a universal service may be selectively financed through the fiscal system. Hence a universal service may in practice not conform to the image conjured up by the notion of a benefit provided for rich and poor alike. Moreover, there are signs of positive discrimination in favour of whole areas of need in such fiscal devices as the Rate Support Grant, the tax credits scheme, and the educational priority areas, although in the past selectivity worked in favour of the well-to-do. This explains in part the suspicion with which the principle of selectivity is regarded by many politicians and publicists.[26]

This is not the place in which to follow all the many and sometimes tortuous arguments in the discussion, in which not only questions of eligibility are involved, but also charges for services, incentives, the widening of choice for the citizen, the reduction of waste and many other matters.

Although the Labour Party's advocacy of universality had originally stemmed from a strong desire among the lower income groups to get away from the hated means test associated with the poor law, the discussion soon developed into an argument that a major purpose of the welfare services is to promote social equality and this can only be achieved if they are available to everyone on the same terms. Mr Crosland, however, in his influential book, *The Future of Socialism*, pointed out that it is only in the services in kind, such as education and health, that a direct link with social equality can be detected. While services must be universally available in order to promote this aim, it is not necessary that they should be free for everyone. A means test for cash benefits is ruled out because the benefits are so essential, and so large in relation to the recipient's means, that he may properly consider he has a social right to them.[27] In general, however, Mr Crosland declared that the ultimate purpose of the social services should be the relief of social distress and hardship, and the correction of social need, while social equality would remain an important subsidiary objective.[28] Furthermore, he contended that much social distress is the result not just of primary and secondary poverty, but may arise from many other individual or familial causes. We should, therefore, devote more attention to the needs of persons suffering from social and psychological defects rather than to the economic causes of distress.[29]

The movement of opinion in the Labour movement since Crosland wrote has been to emphasise the ever-growing need for social and economic equality and to use the welfare services as instruments for achieving it. The creation of comprehensive secondary education in place of grammar schools and secondary modern schools;[30] the threat to transform direct grant schools into ordinary provided schools; the proposal to penalise and possibly extinguish public schools by imposing severe fiscal penalties or integration – are leading examples of efforts to induce more and more parents to send their children to the same school as their neighbours. It is assumed that whatever social or economic differences may exist between individual children and their home environment, the school will act as the melting pot.

The battlecry in the sphere of education was to achieve greater equality of opportunity for the underprivileged children who attend primary schools and the much smaller number who were admitted to selective secondary schools within the state system. The search for 'parity of esteem' was applied to schools, but its basic aim was to upgrade the less able pupils. It was originally intended to demonstrate that primary school teachers were entitled to the same status and remuneration as secondary school teachers. A faint-hearted attempt was later made to apply it to the three categories of secondary schools designated as grammar, modern and technical. This proved difficult to achieve and was abandoned in favour of the comprehensive principle. Differences in the abilities of children would no longer be shown by segregating them in different types of school.

The effort to use the education system as a means of producing greater equality of opportunity was applied with even greater vigour to higher education. Twenty-six new universities have been created since 1945 compared with only nineteen which existed before the Second World War, and the number of full-time students increased from about 50,000 in 1938–9 to 235,556 in 1970–1. In addition, twenty-six polytechnics have been established providing full-time, part-time and sandwich courses at all levels of education; and by 1971, 111,283 of their students out of a total of 145,494 were taking advanced courses. These developments were a spectacular demonstration of the speed with which public policy in the welfare state could break down the barriers which had hitherto confined higher education to a small privileged class. The huge expansion of teaching facilities of all kinds had been accompanied by an equally remarkable expansion of grants to students to cover living expenses, fees, books, etc.

Democratic nations have found by experience that excessive inequalities of wealth, privilege and status are incompatible with democracy because they produce inequalities of economic power and political influence. They also set up barriers of class, manners, taste, speech and attitudes which make social intercourse difficult or impossible. For these reasons the rise of socialism in Western Europe after the First World War caused an emphasis to be placed on equality as an end in itself. Social or economic inequality was denounced as unjust and immoral; disparities of wealth or status were bitterly attacked, and equal rights and opportunities were demanded for all.

This trend of thought had a profound effect on the fiscal policy of the welfare state. It led to the imposition of extremely high death duties on the larger estates (although with many opportunities to avoid paying them); to a progressive income tax with an exceptionally high marginal rate on the higher incomes. The ostensible object of these measures was to level down; to establish a ceiling as well as a national minimum. In practice these policies have had a limited effect; and this has led to a demand for more efficacious measures, such as a tax on wealth, on gifts and a tax on inheritance.

The social services have developed in so many directions that it is no longer possible to define them in terms of their original object of establishing a national minimum standard of life below which no one should be permitted to fall. We can see this if we consider the broad purpose of the social services which form an important part of every developed welfare state. One of the primary aims has been the better protection of personal rights, both social and economic. The protection of children, for example, is the purpose of a mass of legislation which safeguards or rescues children from neglect, abandonment, cruelty, commercial exploitation, and other evils. We have legislation to protect adult workers of both sexes from conditions injurious to their health and welfare or endangering their lives in factories, mines, offices or shops. And there are many other protective services.

A second group of social services aims at the rehabilitation of injured, derelict, disabled or handicapped persons. A welfare state must provide for the training or education of persons suffering from blindness, deafness and other handicaps so as to enable them to lead useful lives in occupations for which they are suited; and they may need help in their daily existence. The state provides various types of training centres for disabled persons, and requires firms to employ a specified proportion of disabled persons for work which they are capable of doing. The retraining and rehabilitation of injured persons is another effort in the same direction. Services of this kind, if they are conducted with imagination, knowledge and understanding, can alleviate a vast amount of human suffering and frustration.

A third group of services consists of those which are essentially a form of national investment in the young. The system of publicly administered or publicly financed education is an investment of this kind, the purpose of which can be briefly described as the production of well-educated, alert, intelligent citizens whose innate abilities have been developed and enhanced.

A fourth group of services comprise those which aim at the prevention and cure of sickness. This was the original aim of the public health movement and it remains of fundamental importance. It is now giving way to a more positive concept, namely the attainment of health at all ages and stages of life for the whole nation. The public health movement began with control over the physical environment by such means as the provision of underground sewers and a pure water supply. It proceeded to vaccination and immunisation, and the isolation and treatment of persons suffering from infectious diseases. Then came the medical care of persons suffering from other specific diseases such as tuberculosis or venereal disease, followed by maternity and child welfare work. Out of these separate threads we have woven a comprehensive health service providing medical treatment of every kind.

It is interesting to observe that control over the physical environment has now regained a prominent position in the public health movement with the newly-awakened concern about the many different forms of pollution. Another turn of the wheel is shown by the fact that while in the years between the two World Wars malnutrition was a cause of anxiety to school medical officers, today the obesity of the young is a matter which attracts the serious attention of the medical profession.

The recognition that birth control and abortion form an important part of the functions of the National Health Service is the result of a radical change in public opinion and public policy on the subject of population, sexual relations, and the rights of women. There are several non-medical aspects of these matters, but the point to note here is that the scope of this social service has changed drastically in the last twenty years or so; that its work affects the welfare of the entire nation; and that many of its activities are not directed specifically at the poor or needy, and are not deliberately redistributive.

A fifth group of social services is directed towards fostering the arts and the provision of recreational facilities. Public art galleries, museums and libraries have existed for centuries, but today the modern state is providing encouragement, financial support, facilities and buildings for music, drama, opera, ballet, cinema, broadcasting and television.

The major reason for the expansion of state interest in the arts is a belief that appreciation of our culture is an essential part of welfare. There may be other reasons, such as the desire to demonstrate to the outside world the superior quality of the national culture, and the desire to attract tourists. But the welfare motive is dominant.

The provision of national parks, nature reserves, bird sanctuaries, and facilities for sports and athletics has also become part of welfare policy.

Outdoor recreational facilities are provided, or financed by, the state partly because exercise in the open air is favoured as conducive to health, partly because a policy of full enjoyment is now considered to be almost as important as a policy of full employment, partly because catering for leisure-time pursuits is now seen as an essential ingredient of welfare. There may here too be other motives, such as the desire to achieve prowess in international athletics or sports competitions which are treasured by governments for their prestige value. National parks and nature reserves, also attract tourists.

Social security is an essential part of the welfare state. Social security is a complex idea. It includes a system of social insurance to ensure that those who suffer the financial hardship caused in most cases by unemployment, sickness, death, orphanage, widowhood, invalidity and so forth, shall be entitled to receive specified monetary benefits as a right when these vicissitudes occur. It involves also a social assistance service to look after the needs of those who require help owing to an exceptional emergency or because they are not qualified to receive social insurance benefits or in order to supplement the latter.

In addition to these remedial measures the welfare state is now expected to intervene in the economy in order to prevent unemployment and various other ills from occurring, as I shall explain in Chapter VII.

Public housing is so important a part of national policy that one could almost determine the claim of a country to be recognised as a welfare state by the magnitude of its effort in this sphere in relation to the total demand for housing – except that to do so would mean that the communist countries of Eastern Europe would rank as welfare states despite the fact that their intolerant, totalitarian policies would disqualify them from assuming that status.

Of all the social services the one usually named as 'welfare'[31] has the widest scope, for it covers almost everyone in need, from unmarried mothers to deprived children, from old persons unable to look after themselves to deserted wives with dependent children, from ex-prisoners unable to obtain work to physically or mentally handicapped adults, from homeless immigrants to problem families. The welfare departments provide a wide range of services in cash and in kind to these and other categories of persons who are in need.

The social services are relatively modern in their present form and they play a part of large and growing importance in the life of the community. They contribute vastly to the health, knowledge, ability and welfare of the citizens and are sometimes redistributive. Most of the benefits they yield could not be effectively provided by any other means. There are, of course, private or independent schools; there are privately owned and administered hospitals and clinics; there is a substantial amount of medical practice in the private sector. But only national systems of education, or health services administered by public authorities, can ensure that acceptable standards of knowledge and health are attained by the mass of the citizens. Even if poor families were to be given financial assistance they might not spend it on schools and doctors if they were free to decide. For this reason services in kind, available to everyone, are more effective than offering money to the low income groups as an alternative.

The position in regard to housing is somewhat different. A large proportion of dwellings in the non-communist world are built and owned by the private sector. The house or flat is provided either by the owner for his personal use, or by a builder or development company seeking profit, or by a co-operative enterprise for its members, or by an employer for his employees. But it is universally true that not even in the wealthiest countries, such as Sweden or the United States, have the low income groups been able to obtain dwellings of an acceptable standard – and sometimes not of any standard – through the market. Everywhere the state has had to intervene either with subsidies or with positive methods of ensuring construction at rents within the means of the low income groups. In few, if any, countries has an adequate amount of such accommodation been provided, but the number of slum-dwellers and homeless families, and the amount of overcrowding has diminshed and would be far greater if there had been no state action in this sphere.

We come finally to town and country planning, and its projection on a larger scale in the form of regional planning. This is not generally regarded as a social service, mainly because the potential benefits it can yield are not conferred on individuals but on communities and the environment. Yet since town and country planning aims at preventing or rectifying overcrowding, squalor, bad housing, lack of amenities, an insanitary or unpleasant environment, poor communications, etc., it has an incontestable claim to be regarded as part of the state's welfare policy. One cannot imagine a welfare state which does not vigorously undertake town and country planning and regional planning.

NOTES

1 A brilliant account of this movement is contained in Beatrice Webb's *My Apprenticeship* (1926), Chapters 4 and 5.
2 *The Necessary Basis of Society* (1908), pp. 11–12.
3 Beatrice Webb, *Our Partnership* (1948), p. 482.
4 Richard M. Titmuss, *Commitment to Welfare* (1968), pp. 85–6.
5 D. C. Marsh, *The Welfare State* (1970), p. 8.

6 B. Abel-Smith, 'Whose Welfare State?' in Norman Mackenzie (ed.), *Conviction* (1958), p. 58.
7 J. V. T. Baker, 'Social Services and Economic Development', in K. J. Scott (ed.), *Welfare in New Zealand* (1955), pp. 88–9.
8 *Towards Equality* (1971), p. 89.
9 'The Place of Values in Social Policy', *Journal of Social Policy* (January 1972).
10 G. Tegner, *Social Security in Sweden* (1956), p. 16.
11 Richard M. Titmuss, *Essays on the Welfare State* (1958), p. 39.
12 Titmuss, *Commitment to Welfare* pp. 64–5.
13 Titmuss, *Essays on the Welfare State*, pp. 40–1.
14 P. Heinig, 'Social Services and Public Expenditure in Sweden', *Industrial and Labour Review* (July 1960), pp. 536–7; Tegner, op. cit., pp. 26–7.
15 Marsh, op. cit., p. 5.
16 'Taxation and Redistribution in the United Kingdom', *Review of Economics and Statistics* (August 1950), p. 206.
17 *The Social Services: Needs and Means* (1952), p. 5.
18 *The Constitution of Liberty* (1960), p. 289.
19 ibid., p. 303.
20 Andrew Shonfield expressed the opinion that to consider the sole purpose of social welfare services to be the establishment of a minimum living standard below which no one should fall is a conception of welfare derived from the traditional notion of charity. It may be regarded as a way of eliminating private acts of philanthropy to relieve poverty by transferring them to the state. *Modern Capitalism* (1965), p. 93.
21 'The Labour Party and Social Services', *Political Quarterly*, Vol. 24 (January–March 1953), p. 66.
22 Hayek, op. cit., p. 303.
23 MacLeod and Powell, op. cit., p. 10.
24 *Commitment to Welfare*, p. 134.
25 R. Mendelsohn, *Social Security in the British Commonwealth* (1954), p. 61.
26 Mike Reddin, 'Universality versus Selectivity', in William A. Robson and Bernard Crick (eds), *The Future of the Social Services* (1970), pp. 22–35.
27 Anthony Crosland, *The Future of Socialism* (1956), pp. 143–5.
28 ibid., p. 147.
29 ibid., pp. 155–6.
30 R. Bilski, 'Ideology and the Comprehensive School', *Political Quarterly*, Vol. 44 (June 1973).
31 There is now a tendency to replace this name by the expression 'personal social services'.

Chapter III

Social Attitudes
in the Welfare State

The question I shall discuss in this chapter is whether the pre-vailing attitudes and outlook in Britain today are compatible with the principles and policies of the welfare state. This is at once the most intangible and the most important issue of our time.

The welfare state was born in an era of moral shock and remorse caused by the revelation of the appalling conditions among the poor shown to exist by Charles Booth's great inquiry into the *Life and Labour of the People of London*, and other investigations. A sense of compassion combined with the pangs of conscience led to a middle- and upper-class revolt against a state of affairs which had now become intolerable. A widespread feeling of shock and compassion for the helpless victims of circumstances beyond their control again erupted during the period of mass unemployment in the years between the two World Wars, and especially during the great depression. Little of that moral or emotional climate still exists.

Gunnar Myrdal has expressed the view that human solidarity and compassion towards the needy are the only motives that can effectively appeal to the people of developed nations.[1] Neither seems to be much in evidence nowadays either in Sweden or in Britain. We were told nearly two decades ago that in Sweden social policy had developed into a vested interest for strongly organised groups, especially those representing labour and management.[2] Everyone in Britain has for some years been unpleasantly aware of the fact that the power to make the public suffer is the most important factor in collective bargaining and the chief weapon in both official and unofficial strikes.[3] The colder the weather the more effective will be the miners' strike or the electricity workers' go-slow; the nearer the peak holiday season the more favourable is the moment for disrupting the travel services by working to rule.

Human solidarity is often seen to be lacking even among the wage earners. Many trade disputes today affecting a small group of skilled workers will put at risk the jobs of thousands of their fellow workers. The dispute at Chrysler in 1973 arose from a refusal by the management to concede a claim by 160 electricians to £5 a week, which the company declared was above the legal limit imposed by the Government. The Company repeatedly said that if this strike continued the plant at Linwood would be closed down, thereby causing 7,000 men to lose their employment. A similar situation existed at the Girling works in Merseyside in 1975 when 5 setters were sent home: 22 others walked out and this led to 400 men being laid off, and eventually 5,000 workers at Fords and Rover being out of work.[4]

Each of the major political parties accuses the other of introducing or advocating policies which would divide the nation to a greater extent than it is at present. The budget is a favourite occasion for allegations of this kind. The public schools are denounced because of their divisive results in terms of class, and the Labour Party has decided to abolish the grammar schools because the selection of pupils according to intellectual criteria is said to be divisive. Militancy and conflict are clearly divisive, yet a university lecturer not only regards their emergence as 'a tool in social manipulation' but urges the so-called 'clients' of the social services to adopt a militant policy.[5] Amid these and other disruptive influences it is difficult to see forces of equal strength working for unity in the nation. Yet without a large measure of unity can we have a welfare society? Today the air is filled with loud cries of protest, denunciation, anger and conflict.[6] The mobilisation of grievances has become the dominant feature of British politics.

Compassion still exists, or can be evoked, as the case of the thalidomide children showed, to compel effective action which would not otherwise have taken place. There is a vast amount of both voluntary and vocational work being carried out for a multitude of different causes by men and women whose chief motive is compassion. But compassion plays a rather small part in the formation of public policy nowadays: the loudly proclaimed concern of the politicians for the old-age pensioners is a thinly disguised attempt to attract the millions of votes which they command.

Society in Britain nowadays is largely a selfish society, observed Lord George-Brown in his autobiography. 'Maybe this is an inevitable phase – first, you make people physically and financially better off, and then you have to wait for human understanding and compassion to catch up.'[7] This is an optimistic view, for lost sympathy is hard to regain. There is no logical reason why human understanding and compassion should 'catch up' with the improved material conditions of people who have lost interest in those who are less well off. The most unpopular act of the Labour Government of which George Brown was a leading member was, he writes, the clawback of family allowances from the better-off taxpayers through income tax. He also mentions the resistance and resentment to taxation on high earnings[8] now felt by all classes.

Lord George-Brown attributes the decline in compassion partly to the lack of idealism in the Labour Party's election campaign of 1970. 'Any left-wing party, any radical party, has got to be a party of idealism and change. Our failure in 1970 was we didn't offer enough idealism. I think, perhaps, we wanted too much to stay in power.'[9] Even selfish people, he thinks, can be swayed by aspirations.

But altruism must have a basis of ideas. Is there not a void in the realm of creative thought relevant to the social and political conditions of our age? Iris Murdoch, in a perceptive essay, declares that the working-class movement which produced socialist theory no longer exists, whereas the trade union movement does exist. The trade unions are interested only in material gains for their members and, as she puts it, 'it is impossible to call up moral visions in a situation in which there is no material incentive to make people lift their eyes to the hills'.[10] The void in our thinking about moral and social problems is compounded by the decline not only in the influence of religion as a guide, but also of other creeds such as socialism, communism, pacifism and internationalism, which for a time served as substitutes for religion.[11]

The dearth of new political thought is not peculiar to the Labour movement. It is equally true of the Conservative and Liberal parties, and also of the intellectual world generally. Political scientists have not provided a theory of the proper province of state action in the contemporary world. We have, as Professor Self recently pointed out, little more than the traditional liberalism of Locke and John Stuart Mill combined with the socialistic framework laid down by Harold Laski in his *Grammar of Politics* as a political philosophy for an era in which the functions and aims of the state have widened almost beyond recognition. The term welfare state offers no guide to the proper limits of individual freedom or governmental action.[12]

The principal watchword which is now invoked to justify welfare policies is equality. It has to serve for validating proposals or decisions in the fields of education, health, housing, taxation, sex relations, the position of women in society and much else. To advocate equality has become the conventional wisdom of the Left. The question which is seldom asked is how widespread in practice is the belief in equality – and in particular in economic equality. The trade unions support demands for equality to be achieved through the political machinery of the state. But they fight incessantly for the maintenance of inequality for their own members. This inequality is disguised under the name of differentials.

The principle of political equality is generally accepted today in Britain. The principle of social equality has never been as fully accepted in these islands as in the United States, partly because we have never completely shed the deference to titles of nobility which are a heritage of feudalism, and partly because of widespread snobbery. Better educational opportunities have in recent years resulted in greater social equality; but the arrival of a substantial contingent of coloured immigrants has raised a new and dangerous challenge. It is, however, in the economic context that it is most difficult to believe that the principle of equality receives widespread support from the nation, except in regard to the use of political measures intended to level up and level down. In the vast realm where private initiative and personal desires reign supreme we see the great popularity of premium bonds offering the chance of large money prizes; the huge appeal of football coupons offering untold wealth to those lucky in their forecasts; we see men and women of all classes crowding the bingo halls and the betting shops; while the heroes of the younger generation are the pop stars who are able to earn fabulous incomes despite a minimum of training or musical talent. The practice of 'lumping' in the building trade, deplored by unions and employers alike, was not a method devised by those devoted to the principle of equality.

The resistance to equality of treatment for women has been most marked in the economic field. While men are sharing with their wives the domestic tasks in the home to a greater extent than ever before, and are ready to take an active part in the care of young children, and while the double standard in sexual conduct has almost disappeared, progress on the economic front has been extremely slow. London Transport was not permitted by the trade unions to engage women bus drivers until October 1973 despite a continued shortage of drivers. Women booking clerks appeared on the railways only very recently. Women engineers are not to be found in British factories. No woman newscaster had appeared on BBC radio or television until 1974. Women medical students have been limited by a secret *numerous clausus* which normally limited them to 15 per cent of the total intake. Women were banned from the London Stock Exchange until 1973, and they have only a tiny smattering of places on the bench and at the Bar. They have been subjected to substantial discrimination in the Civil Service and in the Foreign Service. They are not ordained as priests in any of the churches.

Such phenomena are not found only in Britain. A working group on equality set up in 1969 by the Swedish Democratic Party and the Swedish Confederation of Trade Unions covered almost every aspect of the subject, including the labour market, education, the family, the law, society and employees. The report recorded that great progress had been made in recent decades in many directions but stated that women who work have to be satisfied with subordinate and low-wage employment, although women's earnings are gradually rising in relation to men's. On the broader issue the Alva Myrdal report has this to say: 'Wage policy is vital to the achievement of the Social Democrats' goal of equality. Opposition has been very strong both from market forces and from "institutional" factors, especially trade unions in the higher wage brackets.'[13] The report advocates a transformation in the determination of wages and salaries. Work requiring most knowledge and training is likely to be more stimulating, while the absence of intellectual requirement makes work monotonous and boring, and the degree of pleasure or displeasure should be reflected in the remuneration. The need for special abilities and intelligence should not be overrated and 'the real effort', both physical and mental, accorded a higher place in fixing wage levels. The length of education and training, the value of labour, and its supply in relation to demand, would apparently play little part in this policy.[14]

A conspicuous feature of the contemporary social climate is the emphasis placed on citizen rights and the almost total omission of citizen duties. Every child has a right to be educated at the public expense to the highest point he is capable of attaining; he has the right to be trained at public expense as a doctor or a scientist or an engineer. He then has the right to emigrate to the United States or anywhere else where he can earn a higher income or find better conditions or lower taxation and avoid the restrictions of the welfare state. Every worker has a right to withhold his labour at any moment, with or without the support of his union, and to have his wife and children supported by payments from the Supplementary Benefits Commission. Every director of a company has had the right to have his fees or salary paid to his account in an island tax-haven.[15] The lack of concern about the duties which the citizen owes to the state is having a debilitating effect on the nation, since it often results in a moral vacuum. Unless civil rights are complemented by civil duties we cannot have a welfare society.

This raises the question of responsibility. In Victorian and Edwardian days there was untold misery of every kind among the working class: malnutrition and undernourishment, sickness and premature death, atrocious working conditions, slums and cellar dwellings, child labour and many other evils abounded. The almost incredible indifference of the middle and higher ranks of society to this vast mass of suffering prior to the revelations by Charles Booth and official investigations was a form of irresponsibility. Now it appears that the compassion which led to the creation of the social services has helped to spread a different kind of irresponsibility.[16] For example, on compassionate grounds payments are made out of public money to support deserted wives, unmarried mothers, and the families of men who may have robbed banks of vast sums of money. The desire to prevent innocent suffering in such circumstances has been regarded as far more important than any possible weakening of a sense of responsibility – which might not exist in any event. Helping children attending state schools is alleged to weaken the parents' sense of responsibility; but so too does the practice of the richer parents who send their children to expensive public boarding schools. Such contentions are often nicely balanced, and the evidence for one policy or the other so tenuous that no objective conclusions can be drawn.

There are, however, areas in which the question of responsibility has become of crucial importance. One of them concerns incomes and prices, now recognised to be a matter of the highest importance to the economy. In a country such as Britain, in which every industry, profession, trade, category of workpeople, technicians or managers, is strongly organised usually on a national scale, it is possible for many of these organisations to disrupt the economy if they push their claims to the extreme point of taking industrial action. This indeed has been demonstrated *ad nauseam* during the past decade and has played havoc with the economy. Our system of industrial relations – if it can be called a system – appears to resemble a jungle. Moreover, it is not only the private sector of the economy which has suffered from these self-inflicted wounds. For the first time in our history we have had strikes in the Post Office, the Civil Service, the municipal services and in the municipal schools. Consultants and junior doctors in the National Health Service have embarked on their version of a go-slow or work to rule.

For such a state of affairs to exist as a chronic condition of industry, whether publicly or privately owned, and also in the public services both central and local, indicates a lack of responsibility on the part of the parties to the negotiating processes which is necessary to ensure the smooth working of the economy. It would be absurd to ascribe blame in any generalised way. In some instances the fault lies with the management of a particular firm, in others with the employers' association, in others again with the trade union or unions concerned, and yet others with the government or a public corporation. What is incontestable is that in a country which is more dependent than almost any other for its livelihood on foreign trade, and in which economic growth is declared to be a major national objective, the continual occurrence of stoppages of work due to industrial disputes affecting major industries or services, or even the entire economy, are clear signs that irresponsible attitudes are prevalent among the parties involved; and such attitudes are not compatible with a welfare society. Arguments about the inevitability of conflict are on a par with those about the inevitability of governmental corruption in the United States or in developing countries. Whether inevitable or not, they are adverse elements which cannot be reconciled with the needs of a welfare society.

Professor Ben Roberts concedes that collective bargaining has the merit of legitimising decisions which resolve differences of interest and thereby make them acceptable to those involved. But, he writes,

'Unfortunately it is a method that advances the interest of the strong much better than it protects the weak. The inflationary rates of pay increases have often been not at the expense of employers, but at the expense of the old-age pensioner and the fixed income group. Collective bargaining has failed to change significantly the broad distribution of income. The low paid are relatively as badly off as ever they were. It has taken an Act of Parliament to bring about an improvement in the relative pay of women. Industrial conflict, which has grown steadily over the past twenty years, has brought no general gain in real wages to workers over that which can be attributed to increases in productivity; but the nation as a result of strikes and resistance to change is almost certainly worse off from the loss of production and the discouragement of innovation.'[17]

The Webbs' great works on the history, functions and working methods of trade unions were the first scholarly studies in the subject; but the authors became increasingly sceptical of the value of *laissez-faire* collective bargaining as the best method of determining wages and working conditions. Sidney Webb stated, in an official report, that a strike or lockout necessarily involves so much individual suffering, so much injury to third parties and so much national loss, that it could not in his opinion be accepted as the normal way of settling an intractable dispute. He could not believe that a civilised community would permanently continue to abandon the adjustment of industrial disputes – and incidentally the regulation of the conditions of life of the mass of the people 'to what is, in reality, the arbitrament of war'.[18] The leaders of the trade unions insist with all the emphasis at their command that unfettered collective bargaining between the parties to a dispute, with no holds barred, is the only proper and acceptable method of determining wages and conditions of employment. Such arrangements are appropriate to a *laissez-faire* state; they are certainly not compatible with a welfare society, for in such a society welfare is not only something created by the state through the action of public authorities, but is also generated by the actions and attitudes of individuals, groups, and institutions.

This raises the broad question of freedom and discipline. Industrialism integrates the community. It makes all its members dependent on one another and the different sectors of the economy interdependent. The government and the people are also brought closer together. When an industrialised nation becomes a welfare state the need for a strong sense of individual, group and institutional responsibility and the need for social discipline become far greater because irresponsibility and indiscipline cause disruption, fear and suffering of many different kinds. Airline pilots or ground staff on strike can destroy beyond repair the holiday plans of thousands of families. Takeover bids or mergers can almost without notice deprive thousands of workers of their jobs. Hooliganism by football fans can not only disrupt the game and endanger the players and other spectators but leave a trail of senseless damage and fear in remote towns and villages. Motorists who disregard police warnings in foggy weather can produce a holocaust of death and destruction on motorways.

It would be an exaggeration to suggest that the sense of responsibility has in all respects declined in the past twenty or thirty years. The thalidomide tragedy showed that a leading newspaper, MPs and the shareholders of a great company could compel the directors of a vast commercial corporation to show a much greater sense of humanity and of responsibility towards the victims of a medical disaster than they had displayed during ten years of protracted negotiations. Many young persons, who are most rebellious against authority of all kinds, display a highly developed sense of responsibility towards individuals in need of help. One of the more commendable trends is an increased sense of responsibility for the well-being and humane treatment of animals. On balance, however, it would seem that we are suffering from a substantially diminished sense of responsibility towards our fellow citizens and the community, especially in the economic sphere.

This diminution applies with special emphasis to those who break the criminal law. The traditional crimes of violence against persons and property (murder, assault, rape, arson, etc.) are associated with feelings of sin and guilt, and are sanctioned by strong social sanctions as well as legal penalties. Prisoners who commit offences against children often suffer from the hostility and contempt of their fellow prisoners. The more modern offences such as tax evasion, traffic violation, reckless or dangerous driving, pollution of air, rivers, land or sea, the dumping of noxious chemicals, drug pushing and smuggling, contravention of the food and drugs regulations, do not evoke the same feelings of sin and guilt on the part of those who commit them or the moral condemnation of the general public. Yet these modern crimes are committed on a much larger scale and are in the aggregate far more damaging to society than the traditional crimes of violence against persons and property. They are often committed by well-adjusted and well-to-do persons drawn from all classes of society, as contrasted with the maladjusted, deprived, underprivileged or mentally handicapped individuals who commit many of the traditional crimes. The attitude of public opinion and of society is far more tolerant and the practices of the courts more lenient towards those who commit the modern offences.

But cutting across these distinctions is a strong trend of opinion which tends to remove all personal responsibility from those who display deviant behaviour, however harmful to the victim or to society; to transfer responsibility from the convicted criminal to the social conditions which produced such behaviour, and to the community which permitted them to exist. Thus, the argument declares it is we who are the guilty ones, not those who have committed the crimes.

The erosion of responsibility for criminal behaviour has a long history. Freud unwittingly played a substantial part in the movement of opinion by showing that deviant conduct is often the result of subconscious conflicts, urges and hatreds due to causes of which the actor is unaware and is unable to understand or control. The decline of religion and the dissolution of an accepted moral code in a changing world have been powerful agents in helping to transfer culpability from the criminal to the society which produced him. These same influences have been powerful forces in the evolution of the permissive society, in which pre-marital and extra-marital sexual relations, homosexuality, lesbianism, illegitimacy, venereal disease, drug addiction and possibly incest are seldom subjected to moral condemnation or social disapproval.

Formerly, crowd hysteria was a phenomenon usually manifested by men and women attending mass meetings addressed by well-known evangelical preachers or in the inter-war years by fascist dictators in Germany and Italy. Today, the scene of crowd hysteria is the football match or the pop group. The swaying, chanting football fans may often be in a light hypnotic trance. They feel omnipotent and invulnerable; they experience an oceanic sense of freedom in the crowd. They carry offensive weapons of many kinds. They fight with opposing fans to gain status and esteem. They sometimes rush on to the field during play in a state of frenzy, or throw missiles in order to weaken the defence. On the way home they leave a trail of destruction. Seven Midland doctors who studied the malady urged, *inter alia*, that youth clubs should be attached to every major football club to encourage young people to take a *responsible* interest in the game.[19]

A similar inquiry has not yet been conducted into the mass hysteria exhibited by thousands of teenage girls, sometimes only 10 or 12 years of age, who swoon and scream at the performances, or the arrival and departure of pop groups at hotels, concert halls, airports, etc. Whatever might be the contents of such an inquiry or the nature of its recommendations, we can be sure that the subject would not be considered as having any moral implications. We look for guidance today to the physician, the sociologist, the psychologist and the social worker. So far they have not shown us the way to a welfare society.

Restraints imposed by the state in the alleged interest of morality are regarded with increasing disfavour. The provision disqualifying a woman from receiving a widow's pension if she is cohabiting with a man is criticised as an unjustifiable attempt to interfere with people's sex life, and the officials who inquire into such questions are denounced as snoopers.

The welfare state does not measure social needs by standards of morality. Thus in Sweden an unmarried mother receives a higher benefit than if she were married because her need is greater.[20] All such provision is only possible because the social condemnation of illegitimacy has been replaced by compassion for the child and a concern for the material needs of the mother. The only moral element still remaining is derived from a feeling that the one-parent family is a serious disadvantage for the child, and should therefore be discouraged where possible.

Gambling continues to exert its compulsive attraction to the British people, with less restraint since betting shops were permitted. On the face of it, betting appears to be a harmless activity which is in no way inconsistent with the aims of the welfare state, but on further reflection doubt enters the mind. When millions of wage earners fill in their football coupons each week or buy premium bonds or bet on horse racing or the dogs, they do so in the hope that they will win a prize big enough to enable them to live on an unearned income. The newspapers, radio and television depict the winning bus driver or factory-hand happy in the knowledge that he will in future be able to live in comfort or luxury without having to work for his living. None of his fellow wage earners see anything wrong in the lucky man withdrawing from production and living on the work of others. Their political and trade union leaders do not denounce gambling or ostracise the winners. They confine their criticism to the property owners, the speculators on the Stock Exchange and the take-over promoters who engage in similar activities as part of their regular business. The fact remains, however, that gambling for large prizes through premium bonds or football coupons is inspired by the parasitical dream of the *rentier* which appears to be shared by millions of wage earners and their families.[21] One would like to know how far this attitude has influenced the lack of a serious attitude towards work which is widespread throughout the British economy. Anyone who has visited Japan or the United States or West Germany cannot fail to be impressed by the far greater concentration of interest and attention given to the job to be done than one finds normally in Britain, whether on a building site or in a shop or in a municipal office or the showrooms of a gas or electricity board. Yet we cannot have an adequate welfare state unless there is a more serious attitude to work in the society which sustains it.

Even universities have been criticised on the ground that they do not always reflect welfare concepts. Richard Titmuss cited some negative attitudes to support his contention that they often do not. He mentioned the concept of the teaching 'load' or 'burden' which some teachers feel prevents them from getting on with their own work; the infighting between departments for scarce resources;

the over-expansion of some subjects and the under-development of others; the standard of the examination system and the structure of degrees which are aimed at producing professors and specialists; and the disparagement of teaching and the elevation of research.[22]

Some of these features of British universities may be rubbed off on students, and may help to explain their widespread revolt against many aspects of modern society. This revolt is a world-wide phenomenon though it differs from country to country. Student protest often stems from defects in the educational system of the country concerned.[23]

Students form only a small proportion of discontented young people whose protests attract attention. But student rebels have a special significance, partly because they are the most articulate section of the young, partly because they are well organised, and partly because they will in due course occupy leading positions in many walks of life.

Students in British universities have protested against a great many facets of our society and have demonstrated against many events and governmental policies at home and abroad, such as the Vietnam War, apartheid in South Africa, the Greek military regime, UDI in Rhodesia, the subjugation of Biafra, the Pakistani war on Bangladesh, etc. On home affairs they are against any form of racialism, sex discrimination, successful speculation, homelessness, profiteering, nuclear arms, rocketing prices of land and houses, industrial tycoons, the establishment, 'the City', and, more generally, cruelty, injustice, hypocrisy, underprivilege and oppression. Some of them go much further and oppose materialism, which they see as the progenitor of the consumer society in which welfare is identified with the mass production and distribution of household durables, motor cars and television sets. Most of these attitudes are negative: they indicate what students are against, rather than what they support or advocate. In their attitudes towards cases of individual hardship or group suffering, however, the student response is positive, compassionate, immediate and based on a strong moral concern with the unfortunate, the handicapped, the underprivileged, the old and the sick. These attitudes are essentially compatible with the characteristics of a welfare society, but what is at present lacking among students is any clear idea of the economic, social and political policies or structure which is needed to create and support a welfare state.

A welfare state is not simply a national regime based on a set of objective principles or precepts which after discussion have been embodied in public policies carried out by legislation, central departments and local authorities. Its real force and strength must come from widespread feelings, convictions and responses among the citizens transmitted to their many associations which are consistent with and complementary to those policies. If the pre-vailing feeling is what has been described as 'democratic envy' whereby jealousy and resentment are felt whenever one person has something which others have not got, then the welfare state will generate new social conflicts and incompatibilities. One recalls the campaign during the Attlee administration directed against ministerial motor cars by certain Conservative newspapers and politicians. The campaign of Mr William Hamilton, MP, against the Queen and the royal family appears to aim at arousing social jealousy based on expenditure. At the other extreme is the notion that the primary purpose of social welfare is to help those people who have not achieved a satisfactory position in a career-orientated society.[24]

There is much truth in the suggestion that we have not yet any very clear idea of the direction in which we wish our society to develop. Professor Marsh asks,

'Do we want an "acquisitive society" in which the material rewards go to the few who have the power to divert an undue share of the nation's resources for their own benefit, hence gaining more power and a status very different from the rest of us? Or would we prefer a society in which all had a reasonable share of the nation's resources, and differential rewards were based on responsibilities and contribution to the common good, and equality of opportunity a civic right? . . . And so we could continue theorising about the kind of society we want ours to be, giving it a distinctive label such as "welfare", "acquisitive", "protective", "consumptive", "competitive", "egalitarian", "elitist", "permissive", and the like, but all too often using words without precise meaning or even defined limits.'[25]

In Britain today several of these characteristic qualities exist simultaneously. Capitalist enterprise, from the small shopkeeper to the great multinational company, from the betting shop to the vast joint stock bank, is both acquisitive and competitive. The desire for continuously rising standards of living among wage earners, for example, represents the consumptive element while the insistence of each trade union on common scales of remuneration and of output for their members are examples of group egalitarianism. The system of state education is pinned more and more to an egalitarian pattern, notably with the emphasis on the comprehensive school; while the public schools and Oxbridge tend towards elitism. Compared with the position fifty years ago, we have moved closer to an egalitarian society, but there are still immense economic and social inequalities of many different kinds. How much nearer to equality the nation will wish to go is not clear; but the removal of privilege and the levelling process is the principal battlecry for social reformers or politicians of the Left. I have tried to show that different concepts or conditions co-exist in different parts of the nation. Sometimes they may conflict, and then a choice must be made; but often the different parts of the nation may continue to exhibit different characteristics indefinitely.

Even Sweden, which in many respects is an advanced welfare state, also exhibits some quite different characteristics. A recent Fabian pamphlet asserts that with the possible exception of Belgium, Sweden has the greatest concentration of inherited wealth in Europe. Five per cent of the richest people own a third of the total taxable wealth, and seventeen groups of proprietors control firms employing a fifth of all wage earners in private enterprise. Shareholding is restricted to six per cent of persons in receipt of an income.[26]

What emerges from this part of the analysis is that a continuous effort is needed to eliminate flagrant anomalies; to discover what is or should be the dominant pattern of a welfare society, and to mould the existing policies and institutions to ensure that such a pattern prevails and is not overshadowed by other conflicting patterns; above all, to harmonise the political objectives of state policy with the convictions, activities and aims of the citizens.

It should be clear by now that a welfare society is not concerned solely with the publicly provided social services, or with ensuring a minimum standard of living, or with helping those in need – the old, the sick, the handicapped, the orphans, the destitute, the homeless, the widows and unmarried mothers – or with promoting equality and preventing abuses. It is also concerned with our feelings as individual human beings and with our enjoyment of life.

It is necessary to say this because the social climate in this respect in Britain at the present time appears to be counter-productive so far as these last-mentioned aspects of welfare are concerned. The emphasis on disaster, fear and violence in the press and in broadcasting is a daily phenomenon. The newspaper reader, television viewer or the listener to radio is continuously fed with news, the main items of which consist of war, bombing, rebellion, hijacking, crimes of violence, strikes, earthquakes, railway accidents and similar events. Events in Algeria, Vietnam, Nigeria, Pakistan and the Middle East were reported daily at great length when they were the scenes of fighting, death and destruction. When peace broke out they almost disappeared from the news overnight. How much interest will the mass media take in Northern Ireland when the bombing and shooting stop? Obviously, news must be reported whether it is good or bad, but the obsession with death, violence and disaster presents a one-sided picture of life which has a depressing effect on the reader or viewer. In the totalitarian countries bad news affecting the nation is either suppressed or hidden away. 'Nothing bad ever happens in Spain', a Spanish acquaintance ironically remarked to me; and the same policy of suppressing bad news is observed in the Soviet Union, Poland and other countries in Eastern Europe. It is probable that we have gone to the other extreme.

Mr Marsland Gander, the broadcasting critic, has pleaded for less emphasis on woe, gloom and despondency in broadcasting. His readers have urged that public affairs sessions should not concentrate exclusively on such subjects as strikes, greed, protests and student unrest.[27] No one would wish to live in a fool's paradise or to be prevented from knowing what is going on in the world, whether at home or abroad. It is the morbid obsession with fear, violence and disaster, and the absence of any interest in achievement, success and altruism, except in the field of sport or money-making, which has been and is presenting a biased picture and is creating an atmosphere of pessimism and hopelessness which detracts from a conscious belief in or experience of well-being.

Similar tendencies can be observed in the theatre and the cinema. The plays of Ibsen, Shaw, Galsworthy, Granville Barker, Priestley, Brecht and others dealt with large social or political problems. The contemporary theatre is mainly concerned with situations affecting the relations of a small number of individuals, without wider implications. The typical contemporary play presents a situation of conflict, suffering or misunderstanding which does not change or develop in any significant way and for which no solution is possible. Here again, hopelessness and despair have taken over.

Lord Clark, writing about the reasons for the international success of his television series 'Civilisation' said the short answer was to be found in Wordsworth's lines:

> We live by admiration, hope and love
> And even as these are well and wisely fixed
> In dignity of being we ascend.

That kind of nineteenth-century sentiment is regarded as a joke, observed Lord Clark, for 'a majority of television programmes, films and novels suggest that we live by contempt, hatred and despair. There is no doubt that this expresses the mood of our time, a mood which is easily understood if one thinks about the history of the last 40 years. But admiration, hope and love remain basic human needs.'[28]

The permissive society is an attempt to satisfy some frustrated human needs and to liberate activities formerly restricted, but it does not necessarily bring nearer a world in which it is possible for human beings to experience feelings of admiration, hope and love. I realise that such questions are regarded as entirely outside the legitimate concern of social scientists, who are not supposed to grapple with the problems of human happiness. But confining myself to the narrower sphere of welfare, I maintain that a welfare state, and still more a welfare society, cannot exist in an atmosphere of pessimism, gloom and despondency, in which the human predicament evokes feelings of contempt, hatred and despair. All such generalisations are of course inevitably over-simplifications, but the mental and moral climate of an era is not so nebulous that it defies any attempt at definition or understanding.

In conclusion, while one can detect and identify the prevailing sentiments, it is quite another matter to suggest how they can be changed.

NOTES

1 'The Place of Values in Social Policy', *Journal of Social Policy* (January 1972).
2 G. Tegner, *Social Security in Sweden* (1956), p. 13.
3 E. H. Phelps Brown, 'Collective Bargaining Reconsidered', Stamp Memorial Lecture (1971).
4 Stephen Fay, *Measure for Measure* (1975).
5 Robert Holman in *Socially Deprived Families in Britain* (1973), p. 205.
6 See Bernard Crick and William A. Robson (eds), *Protest and Discontent* (1970), *passim*.
7 *In My Way* (1971), p. 271.
8 ibid., p. 270.
9 ibid., p. 272.
10 'A House of Theory', in *Conviction*, Norman Mackenzie (ed.) (1958), pp. 228–9.
11 ibid., p. 227.
12 'The State versus Man' in *Man and the Social Sciences*, William A. Robson (ed.) (1972), pp. xv–xvi, 63–87.
13 Alva Myrdal, 'Report to the Swedish Social Democratic Party', *Towards Equality* (1971), pp. 27, 35.

14 ibid., pp. 36–7.
15 From 1975 such payments would be liable to UK taxation.
16 N. A. Smith, 'Theory and Practice of the Welfare State', *Political Quarterly*, Vol. 22 (1951), p. 380.
17 'Affluence and Disruption', in Robson (ed.), op. cit., p. 267.
18 ibid., p. 268. The passage occurs in an addendum to the report of the Royal Commission on Trade Disputes 1903–6.
19 'Doctors' Football Cure', *The Times* (26 January 1968).
20 P. Heinig, 'Social Services and Public Expenditure in Sweden', *Industrial and Labour Relations Review* (July 1960), p. 535. An allowance for one-parent families in the United Kingdom is proposed in the report of the Finer Committee on One-Parent Families. HMSO, Cmnd 5629 (1974).
21 Smith, *Political Quarterly*, Vol. 22, pp. 371–2.
22 Richard M. Titmuss, *Commitment to Welfare* (1968), pp. 25–35.
23 Examples drawn from the United States, West Germany, France, Berlin and Rome are given in an article by Richard Davey, 'Distress over Modern Society', *The Times* (1 June 1968).
24 Alva Myrdal Report, *Towards Equality*, p. 91.
25 D. C. Marsh, *The Welfare State* (1970), p. 102.
26 Larry Hufford, *Sweden: The Myth of Socialism*, Young Fabian Pamphlet 33 (1973), p. 1. See also Kurt Samuelsson, *From Great Power to Welfare State* (1968), p. 256.
27 *Daily Telegraph* (11 January 1971).
28 *Radio Times* (11 February 1971), p. 6.

Chapter IV

Equality and Affluence

Some remarks about equality have been made in the previous chapters in relation to the social services, collective bargaining and other matters. In this chapter the focus will be on economic and social equality generally and its relation to affluence.

Many forms of inequality have existed or do exist, such as those resulting from class, sex, race, income and wealth, colour, religion, colonialism, legal status, language, etc. In all of them discrimination has significant economic, social and political consequences. In recent decades, however, economic equality has been a dominant issue in Britain. Nevertheless, other aspects still command attention here and elsewhere, not only by bodies such as Women's Lib but also by a serious inquiry such as that undertaken in Sweden by the Alva Myrdal Committee of the Social Democratic Party.[1]

Mr Douglas Jay asserts that socialists believe in equality as an end. This is not based on the untenable notion that men are born equal but on the moral judgement that everyone has 'as much right as anyone else to whatever gives value to human life',[2] including the right to happiness and civilised life. This is clearly a mistaken view because there cannot be equal rights to love, to the begetting of children, to creative work as a writer, artist or musician, to self-expression as a ballet dancer, champion athlete or sportsman. Jay asks, 'why should I have more right to happiness than you?' One answer may be: because you are better endowed by nature, more lovable, more talented, more fortunate in your parents and genetic inheritance. These differences cannot be eradicated by socialism.

In the end, the rights which everyone should and can possess are political, legal, social and civic: the right to vote, to equality before the law, to hold political office, and other rights which prohibit discrimination based on sex, race, religion, wealth or family background. The state can take positive action to ensure that the natural abilities of every child are fully cultivated in the educational system. It can abolish privilege in the public services and ensure that recruitment and promotion are based on merit. It could prevent or lessen the advantages of family background and social position from exerting the dominant influence which they do today in the foreign service and the higher judiciary. At the other extreme the state could discourage the preservation of the lives of children seen to be suffering at birth from handicaps which will prevent them from ever leading happy or enjoyable lives.

Mr Jay considers that it is the belief in equality which distinguishes socialists from liberals, who share the socialist belief in liberty. Yet whereas in the political, social or legal spheres socialists insist on absolute equality, in the economic sphere very few socialists have ever advocated total equality.[3] Literal equality of incomes is not, he argues, a serious aim because it is unenforceable and impossible to maintain in a free society. The great majority of people, he concedes, including socialists, think the more skilled and diligent workers, and those bearing more responsibility deserve 'a rather greater reward'. Jay also contends that higher rewards are necessary if people of superior knowledge and skill are to use their abilities to the full. He is thus apparently in favour of the market mechanism for invoking maximum effort, qualified by the notion that the aim should be to ensure 'the minimum practicable inequality'. In short, whatever degree of inequality is necessary to induce people to exercise their productive talents for the benefit of society is morally and rationally justified, but nothing above that should be tolerated. How the cut-off point can be identified or defined is not, and probably cannot be, stated; the argument is a purely theoretical one. It is difficult to find any practical guidance from Jay's later statement that the free market will almost always, immediately and cumulatively, produce 'greater inequality than the minimum necessary to get human capacities exercised'.[4] How the minimum is to be discovered is not revealed.

In a later passage the same politician writes that equality of opportunity leads to excessive inequality, unless accompanied by redistribution.[5] It is the free exchange of goods and services, and inheritance of property, and not the ownership of the means of production, which in his view results in cumulative inequality. If we were to nationalise the entire machinery of production, but allowed incomes to be determined and goods to be distributed by market forces, the influence contributing to social injustice would not be seriously affected.[6]

We have already noted that some experts believe that the availability of social services to the entire nation has produced regressive results.[7] 'The middle classes', wrote Professor Abel-Smith in 1958, 'get the lion's share of the public social services, the elephant's share of occupational welfare privileges, and in addition can claim generous allowances to reduce their tax liability.'[8] So, he asks, who has a welfare state? Yet in recent years the middle-class demand for private hospital treatment and fee-paying or public school education for their children has been steadily growing, which looks as though the allegation may be less true than when it was made. It is not certain that it was ever true.

Fiscal policy since the end of the Second World War has not brought about as much redistribution between rich and poor, or between richer and poorer as some people expected. We have recently become aware of the existence of the poverty trap; of the fact that the highest marginal rates of income tax were falling on the poor; that persons with incomes well below the poverty line have been liable to direct taxation. Capital wealth is still concentrated in a relatively small proportion of the population. There has been some redistribution during the present century, but there is no agreement about the extent of the shift. The legally permitted methods of avoiding high death duties have been extensively used by the wealthy classes, with the result that in Britain there is probably greater inequality in the possession of capital wealth than in most countries. Some of these inequalities could be reduced by such devices as a tax on wealth, a tax credit scheme, and a graduated inheritance tax falling on the recipients of bequests.[9]

Attention has usually been concentrated on inequality between classes or income groups. Less interest has been shown in the inequality within classes or income groups, although this can be very severe. In Sweden a major concern of social policy has been to mitigate the hardships arising from family responsibilities.[10] In Britain the scheme of family allowances for children after the first child has had a relatively small influence on family resources compared with the more generous arrangements in France and other countries. Professor Titmuss pointed out long ago that despite all the social benefits in recent years a larger proportion of the national income was being received in most economic groups by those without dependent children.[11] There is no reason to think the position is different today. 'At every income level in our society', wrote Sir Richard Clarke recently, 'the difference between the standard of living of those with and without dependants is very striking, and it is at least as great at the middle-class income levels as at the lower.' He criticises the vertical comparisons often made between family allowances for the poor and income tax reliefs for dependent children as missing an essential point, which is the 'horizontal' comparison between people at the same income levels.[12]

With the disappearance of the great town houses in Mayfair and Belgravia, or their transformation into offices or flats, the handing over of many stately country homes to the National Trust or their conversion into showplaces or museums, and the disappearance of the armies of domestic and outdoor servants employed in maintaining the life-style of their former occupants, inequality is nowadays more obviously displayed in working life than elsewhere in society. Differences in wages or salaries, benefits, status, tenure, working clothes, accommodation, toilet facilities, canteens, and even modes of address, stratify not only working life but the whole nation.[13]

These inequalities are not peculiar to capitalism.[14] They exist on a comparable scale in the Soviet Union, where great disparities of all kinds, including housing, motorcars, incomes and office accommodation, exist between the low paid, unskilled workers and the highly paid scientists, technocrats, party leaders, military commanders, and managers of the great industrial plants and trusts. The latter, like the commissars and the defence chiefs, can also purchase at special shops goods not available to the unprivileged masses. Even in communist China there are millionaires riding around in luxurious cars.[15]

In East Germany the Socialist Unity Party (SED) has stated explicitly that while socialism is the realisation of equal opportunities for all people, it also involves the realisation of the basic principle 'from each according to his ability, to each according to his achievement'.[16] This is a far cry from the Marxian concept of 'to each according to his need'. The salaries of managers differ according to the size and capacity of the enterprise and can be several times as large as the average working wage. Within each enterprise incomes are graded in accordance with the principle of efficiency.[17] Despite these vast differentials the proponents of egalitarianism (for others) are usually identified with communism.

Nonetheless, capitalism does result in practices which not only exacerbate inequalities but are aimed at defeating any progressive objectives the fiscal system may embody. The most notorious are the abuse of the expense account; the upgrading of the standard of 'business' living to a level far above that within the capacity of the employee's private means; the payment of fees and salaries to accounts in islands known to be tax-havens; the provision at the firm's expense of costly motorcars for employees who use them also for private purposes; the purchase of salmon or trout fishing rights ostensibly for the entertainment of customers from overseas, but also used by executives and directors; and many other abuses. By such means high taxation causes what were formerly lavish personal expenditures to be transferred to business expenses.[18]

The situation is one of extreme complexity. In industry and commerce very high salaries are regarded as status symbols of rank and power. But if a man attains a position as chairman or managing director of a large firm at a salary of £50,000 a year, he will certainly believe that he 'earns' that sum and that it is paid not just to the office but because his talents merit a reward on that scale. Men earning high levels of remuneration expect to live in much greater luxury than those with lower incomes; and they will resort to any device which will help them to avoid the tax collector's exorbitant demands. The diversion of a large amount of highly trained, professional brainpower to the task of devising methods of escape from the tax collector's net is not only unproductive but a drain on human resources which could be far better employed in more socially useful work.

Very little is known about the extent to which very high remuneration is necessary to induce men of great ability to exert their talents to the full; and even less about the effect of high direct taxation on incentives to work.[19] Opinions among economists are divided and there is an absence of hard evidence. A widely held belief is that high marginal rates of taxation diminish incentives to work, to accept heavy responsibility, and to incur risks, though the opposite view is sometimes expressed that the more the state takes away from a man, the harder he will work in order to reach the desired level of earnings.

The climate of opinion is now against the extravagant and ostentatious mode of living which existed in Britain among the well-off classes during the reigns of Edward VII and George V. That type of life-style is now more often found on board the big yachts in the Mediterranean or in Bermuda than in Norfolk or Sussex. It has, however, become clear that any substantial degree of redistribution could not be effected by the elimination of the high incomes and wealth but would require a considerable reduction of middle-class incomes and property. This would raise great political difficulties, mainly because public opinion does not condemn middle-class standards of living, and many manual wage earners are now earning middle-class incomes.

Bertrand de Jouvenel has pointed out that the principle of redistribution received its initial impetus by disapproval of two apparently related phenomena: the unrightness of under-consumption and the unrightness of over-consumption.[20] This disapproval still persists, but there is today an increasing awareness that personal incomes are not used only for current consumption but also for the essential function of home building, for the support of art-forms in their early stages of development, and for other socially useful purposes on which public money cannot be spent. The work of Sidney and Beatrice Webb, of Charles Darwin, Carter's archaeological work in Egypt which resulted in the discovery of Tutankhamen's tomb, the full flowering of Bernard Shaw's genius as a playwright, the contribution made by Thomas Beecham to opera and music – these and many other valuable activities were made possible by the possession or support of a moderate amount of private wealth.

'Anything which increases the proportion of fair-booth consumption as against formative expenditure must be adjudged undesirable', writes de Jouvenel. 'Let us by all means turn yachts into county council houses. But it works in the other direction as soon as redistribution cuts into the cultural expenditure of the middle-class to feed the amusement industries.'[21] The difficulty is in discovering a method of discouraging the former and encouraging the latter. Where do we place horse racing, financed by very rich men but enjoyed and supported by the masses in the lower income groups? And why should a Labour government, theoretically devoted to greater equality, be anxious to ensure the continued production of Rolls-Royce motorcars, since their owners will be restricted mainly to film-stars, top business executives and millionaires? The answer is that the pursuit of distributional equality can conflict with the interests of skilled workers producing goods and services for wealthy consumers.

But apart from a conflict of interest of this kind there is also an ambivalent attitude towards expenditure on luxury goods. A militant trade unionist may feel proud of the design and workmanship which produces Rolls-Royce motorcars and also resentful of the ability of rich firms or individuals to buy them. Part of the demand for equality is caused by envy and jealousy, and those who suffer from these emotions derive satisfaction from the levelling down process regardless of its economic or social consequences.

A psychoanalyst has pointed out that the extreme egalitarian may be less concerned with the defence of others than with the destruction of those who make him feel inferior. The feeling of inferiority may be caused by his lack of a feeling of maturity and potency. 'Where this occurs there may be a shift of emphasis from an attack on privilege and power which is used tyrannically to an attack on any individual power above the average whether it is abused or has anti-social results or not. The effect is in any case to transfer more power to the State – and also to centralise such power. The growth of state power may tend to foster the re-emergence of a less mature and more authoritarian morale.'[22]

The reduction of extremes of poverty and wealth are relatively easy to justify. It is the middle ground which presents the most intractable political, economic and social problems; and within the middle ground very great disparities of income and capital can exist. One view is that the welfare state faces an insoluble problem in trying to create equal opportunities while accepting a consider-able degree of social and economic inequality. The problem is likely to be a permanent one because the economic and social position of the family, the material conditions of the home, the attitude of parents towards their children, can all have a significant effect on the child's educational performance and subsequent career.[23] These causes alone – and there are others pressing in the same direction – tend to create increased inequality if nothing is done to counteract them. A determined effort has to be made to maintain even the limited amount of equality we have so far achieved.

An essential aim of the wefare state has been to eliminate poverty by establishing a minimum standard of life below which no one would be permitted to sink. This was the purpose of the Beveridge Report and the legislation which was passed as a consequence of its recommendations. The situation has, however, been radically changed by the fact that few people now accept the notion of poverty originated by Seebohm Rowntree in his studies of York, who defined it in terms of the minimum weekly cost of food, clothing, fuel, household sundries and rent required to maintain a person or a family in a state of physical efficiency.[24] Any family whose total earnings were insufficient to obtain the minimum necessaries, he classified as being in primary poverty. This method was adopted with small adjustments by many of the subsequent studies of poverty in particular areas, and later by Lord Beveridge.

An entirely different approach is now used by several contem-porary writers on the subject of poverty. The notion of a minimum level of subsistence of a more or less fixed character based on physical needs has been superseded by the idea of relative poverty, that is poverty related to the standard of living enjoyed by most people in the community at a specified time. Poverty is now often expressed in terms of relative deprivation, having regard to time and place. Professor Townsend, using this basis, defines individuals, families and groups as being in poverty when 'they lack the resources to obtain the types of diets, participate in the activities and have the living conditions and amenities which are customary, or at least widely encouraged and approved, in the societies to which they belong. Their resources are so seriously below those commanded by the average individual or family that they are, in effect, excluded from ordinary living patterns, customs and activities.'[25] Professor Townsend claims that only by the concept of relative deprivation can poverty be defined objectively and applied consistently. This is a questionable view for several reasons. Is the average family arrived at by considering the whole nation, or a particular city, or a local community? And how clear-cut are the ordinary living patterns, or the customs and activities?

But these are minor criticisms. The basic principle involved in the new formulation appears to be that everyone who is not able to enjoy middle-class standards is assumed to be living in poverty and must be rescued from his state of relative deprivation.

The concept of poverty has not only been raised but has also been widened. Until recently it was formulated in monetary terms, although it was known that the poor had inferior health and education compared with the better-off members of society. But now it is remarked that poverty handicaps people in many other ways. They have less chance of getting decent housing, their prospects in the labour market are inferior, their political influence is low, their chances of rising in the world are small, their children are likely to benefit less from school, and have greater difficulty in finding a promising job than those who come from better backgrounds. The incidence of mental illness is substantially greater in the twilight areas than in the better parts of a city.

The exponents of the new definition of poverty declare that relative deprivation can only be cured by the creation of social and economic equality. This follows logically from their basic premise but it involves a drastic change from the notion that poverty can be abolished by establishing a minimum standard of life for the entire nation. The new definition makes inequality the cause of poverty, and those who would cure it must inevitably advocate the socialist doctrines of egalitarianism. The national minimum concept has been a cornerstone of welfare state policy and the wefare state can scarcely accept so fundamental a change of aim in order to overcome the handicaps of 'the new poor', who by previous standards would in many cases not be living in poverty.

There is much statistical data about the numbers of persons living in poverty at the present time, although most writers agree

that the information is not adequate. But all the estimates show
that the number of persons living on or below the official poverty
line does not exceed more than about 5 per cent of the population,
and some of the estimates could give a much lower figure.[26] But
the significant fact is that even on a generous calculation the poor
are now a small minority of the population, and it is unlikely that
a revolutionary change in the politico-economic regime or a change
in the doctrines of the welfare state will be brought about in the
interests of that particular minority unless it has the support of
the more influential classes of the nation.

Those who believe that the attainment of a substantial degree
of social and economic equality is required in order to eliminate
poverty based on the relative deprivation concept are usually
aware of the magnitude and revolutionary character of the requisite
transformation.[27] They concentrate on the problems of the underprivileged and ignore the wider effects on society in general. They
seldom consider the effect of the transformation on the economy.
Their aim is to abolish the class divisions in British society which
they believe are the main bulwarks of inequality and the principal
causes of poverty.

There is no agreement about the extent to which economic
inequality is necessary for productive efficiency, increased prosperity, capital investment, and a higher standard of living for
everyone, however unequally the benefits may be distributed. The
doctrines of the socialist on this vital question cannot be reconciled with those of the liberal, the free market economist and the
conservative. The attitude of the Labour Party is ambiguous on
this matter, for while ideologically it is committed to egalitarianism,
successive Labour governments have offered the chairmen and
members of the board of nationalised industries salaries far higher
than those previously offered in the public service.

The Select Committee on Nationalised Industries in a report to the
House of Commons declared that the chairmen and board members
of the public corporations must be paid 'a proper rate for the
job'. Their remuneration would be determined by the market,
since the salaries paid by the nationalised industries, compared
with those paid by commercial firms, affect not only the ability of
the public sector to secure the services of people from outside firms,
but also ensure that the nationalised industries will recruit men of
sufficiently high ability to merit promotion to the board. The
predominant objective should be to attract and retain the best
available talent.[28]

The Chairman of the Select Committee was Mr Ian Mikardo,

MP, a left-wing socialist. The report showed that he and other members of the Labour Party were prepared to recommend in the interests of efficiency the introduction of a much higher degree of inequality in the public service than had hitherto existed. It also conceded that persons of exceptional ability must be paid exceptionally high remuneration if they are to exercise their talents for the public good. Most remarkable of all the statements in the report was the assertion that 'insofar as men of high quality are prepared to work in the nationalised industries from a sense of public service, it would be wrong for the State to take advantage of this by paying them a great deal less than they would be paid in comparable posts elsewhere in industry'.[29] It is thus clear that altruism and public spirit are to be excluded from the nationalised industries in favour of the market forces on which capitalism relies. The lesson seems to have been well learnt by the miners, the railwaymen, ambulance drivers, civil servants, school teachers, and other public servants who now frequently withhold their labour on the assumption that the employees of publicly owned industries and services should try to advance or protect their interests by precisely the same methods as those employed in profit-making enterprise. In short, that there is no difference in the motivation of those working in capitalist enterprise or public enterprise so far as self-interest is concerned.

Most people, whatever their political beliefs, would probably agree to the payment of high salaries to men and women of exceptional ability occupying important positions in the public sector if it could be shown that it is necessary to do so in order to recruit and retain them in those jobs. There is, however, no hard evidence at present available to prove or disprove this proposition. It can be contended in any event that a more effective method of achieving a greater degree of economic equality than by equalising salaries is by means of the progressive taxation of inheritance and wealth.

In 1961 Lady Wootton drew attention to the strange neglect of income distribution as an aspect of welfare, and pointed out that only in the matter of wage and salary policy had the rule of *laissez-faire* hitherto survived unchallenged in Britain. The collective bargain, she pointed out, had come to enjoy a remarkable esteem and it was almost blasphemous to question 'if not the divine right of collective bargaining, at least the divine rightness of every collective bargain'.[30] In no other sphere was it accepted that whatever the parties concerned agreed upon is right. In the use of land, in matrimonial and family relations, in working conditions affecting

health and safety, private agreements are subordinate to and
regulated by the public interest. Collective bargaining was 'the
one sphere in which the public interest is thought to require no
protection against private cupidity'.[31]

In her analysis Barbara Wootton showed that the economic
element is often not the determining element in the collective
bargain, and that on the contrary economic changes are resisted
by powerful forces bent on maintaining the traditional patterns:
in short, that *laissez-faire* wage negotiations are highly conservative.
She reached the conclusion that an uncritical acceptance of pre-
vailing relativities is incompatible with the welfare state, since
existing patterns of remuneration do not reflect irresistible economic
realities or considered social judgements applicable to modern
conditions. This applied particularly to the professions. From this
it followed that in a genuine welfare society the social judgements
implied in the existing wage and salary structure would be exposed
to public discussion and challenge.[32]

The most penetrating criticism of our attitudes and ideas about
the distribution of personal incomes has come from Sir Geoffrey
Vickers. He rejects for two reasons the assumption that there is,
or can be, a free labour market. One is that employees are not
regarded either by themselves or by employers as a commodity.
The other is that when a single buyer (whether an employer or an
association of employers) negotiates with a trade union about the
terms and conditions of a collective agreement which neither can
do without for long, they are engaged in an activity which in no
way resembles the process which goes on in a free market. Collective negotiations can be sheer conflicts in which each side tries
by every means in its power to force the other side to give way
by threatening or inflicting serious harm. But although the threat
of coercion may be present, the negotiations are usually attempts
to reach an agreement which takes account of certain limitations
and satisfies certain criteria. These criteria vary according to
circumstances. They may include relativities; or the insistence that
there is a subsistence minimum below which no one's earnings
should fall; or changes in the position of an industry; or the need
to attract and retain more workers or to prevent them from
quitting the industry; or to take account of inflation or increased
productivity; or increased responsibility resulting from changes in
equipment and technology. But over and above such factors are
the conflicts arising from incompatible ethical expectations about
what people feel is fair or due to them or to others.[33]

Sir Geoffrey Vickers takes a gloomy view about the ability of our system of collective bargaining to achieve 'the minimal requirements of a sufficiently stable system' to sustain the economy, to ensure the allocation of adequate resources to investment, and to provide enough revenue for the state to be able to undertake the greatly expanded functions which are demanded. The minimal requirements are 'that total demand shall not exceed the total sum available for distribution; that changes of differentials shall not create more instability than they cure; that whatever procedures are invoked to settle changes shall not be unacceptably costly; and that the end result shall provide acceptably for those not in work as well as for those in work and shall acceptably relate the two'.[34] None of these requirements is met at present. To satisfy them would involve changes in the expectations of government, business and organised labour, and those changes would refer both to their own expectations and those of the other parties to the process of settling claims, for it is people's expectations which determine what they regard as acceptable or unacceptable. This change would mean that many politicians, company directors, business executives, trade union officials, shareholders, men and women on the factory floor, clerks, salesmen, civil servants and professional people, must be prepared to make or accept decisions which may have adverse effects on themselves. Such a change of outlook would have to be made not just by a small group of leaders but by almost everyone, since small dissenting minorities can often block a much wider consensus.

Few people today realise the immense change of outlook and of roles in the bargaining process which will be called for if we are to reduce substantially the great inequalities of income in our society or to abolish the poverty which still exists.

Much has happened since the publication of Lady Wootton's notable contribution. We have seen a Labour government introduce the statutory regulation of remuneration carried out by the National Board for Prices and Incomes, which made recommendations not only for wage earners but also for the salaries of chairmen, chief executives and others in both the private sector and nationalised industry, who are not within the scope of collective bargaining. We have seen that system dismantled by the government which introduced it, and the principles it embodied rejected by a Conservative government. We have seen the Conservative government subsequently introduce a more complex and comprehensive system of income regulation, with different methods of determination and enforcement. All these attempts to inject public policies into the collective bargaining process have been fiercely and persistently resisted by the trade unions and the TUC who declare that the only fair and proper method is by free collective bargaining. The authority of the state and the legitimacy of Parliament have been challenged again and again by trade unions directed by militant leaders, supported by Members of Parliament who are supposed to be left-wing.

The outcome of this struggle is not clear; but what is certain is that *laissez-faire* collective bargaining cannot result in a welfare society, for in such a society the claims or the deserts of groups or individuals would not depend for their recognition on the power which can be mobilised behind those claims – in particular the power to disrupt the economy, to impede social services, and to cause hardship to the consumers or the general public. Moreover, *laissez-faire* collective bargaining tends to increase economic inequality rather than to lessen it, as trade union leaders well know. It would, however, be hard to find a trade union leader or a shop steward, no matter whether he regards himself as a communist or a Trotskyite or a follower of Mao Tse-Tung, who would agree that *laissez-faire* collective bargaining and striking is incompatible with a socialist economy, a welfare state or a welfare society. Among other things such *laissez-faire* activities rule out the possibility of determining collectively the rate of saving.[35] Moreover, wages must be publicly regulated if inflation is to be controlled.

There is, as Professor Marshall points out, a vast difference between a society based on the assumption that free competition and individual enterprise are the highest goods and that the right to possess whatever can be acquired by these means is morally, legally and politically justified, and a society based on the principle that social justice is essential to the concept of legitimacy.[36] The underlying philosophy of the former is that of the affluent society; the philosophy of the latter is that of the welfare state. There are profound differences between them but the contrast is not absolute. A welfare state can be affluent, as Sweden has shown; and every affluent society makes some provision for welfare. But many conflicts arise when the two philosophies exist side by side in a single society which is regarded by some of its members as a welfare state and by others as an affluent society when in fact it is neither.

More realistically, the British nation is not divided in this way. It consists of large numbers of people who are pursuing the aims of an affluent society within the framework of a welfare state. As businessmen, financiers, property developers, industrialists, organised wage-earners, trade union officials, entrepreneurs, shopkeepers, financial journalists, advertising agents, etc., they accept the philosophy of the affluent society and pursue its self-regarding aims with the utmost vigour and complete indifference to questions of social justice and the common good. As consumers, shoppers, passengers on public transport, patients in hospitals and in the doctor's waiting-room, as parents of children in state schools, as private motorists, the pursuit of their own private goal is the dominant concern, but a sense of what the government has or has not done, or should have done, to improve conditions or provide a better service is perceived as relevant. As citizens, the general interest will loom very large indeed. A general election or a local election will be fought on matters of widespread concern, questions of social justice and injustice will figure prominently in the programme of every party, and the programmes will all, in their different ways, claim to be seeking to promote the general welfare and often in addition the welfare of groups in special need, such as the handicapped or the mentally ill, the homeless, the slum-dwellers, the old-age pensioners, or the unemployed. The management of the economy, economic growth, assistance for the development areas, will very likely also occupy a prominent place in the public debate. It is at the political level – and only at that level – that the philosophy of the welfare state is manifested. In the sphere of private enterprise, the Stock Exchange, industrial relations in all sectors, and property development, the values of the affluent society reign supreme.

We speak of the welfare *state* and of the affluent *society*. The distinction in the terms used is because we think of the former as mainly dependent on governmental action whereas the latter is mainly concerned with the actions and outlook of individuals and of commercial companies. There are, however, a large number of non-governmental, non-commercial bodies which make a substantial contribution to the welfare of our society. The Royal Society for the Prevention of Cruelty to Children is one example out of many thousands.

In dealing with animals there is less of a contrast between public policy and private action than in our treatment of fellow human beings. There are laws prohibiting cruelty to animals and regulations to preserve species of birds or mammals in danger of extinction. Vivisection is regulated with some care to prevent unnecessary suffering. The great majority of persons who own pets, whether they are cats, dogs, birds or fish, treat them with affection and kindness. There are of course exceptions. Some of the legislation is grossly inadequate – the regulation of factory farming is an example – and some individuals are guilty of acts of great

cruelty to animals. But on the whole there is a remarkable degree
of consistency in private attitudes and public policies towards
animals and a consensus of aims and values, except in regard
to blood sports. Yet hunters seek to justify their sports by asserting
that they do not cause unnecessary suffering, and stag-hunters
declare that their activities actually prevent much greater suffering.
I am not concerned with the truth or falsity of such statements but
only to show how widespread is the sentiment in favour of the
humane treatment of animals.

The affluent society is a rich society, but it is not necessarily a
society which has abolished poverty or even made a serious attempt
to do so, as the example of the United States clearly shows. Moreover, the affluent society may be one in which public expenditure
and investment on welfare services are minimal, or at least grossly
inadequate, as in the United States and in Japan.

Professor Galbraith has described eloquently the contrast in
America between private affluence and public squalor. He defines
the fundamental characteristics of the affluent society as an
obsession with production accompanied by the artificial stimulation
of consumption which is necessary in order to absorb the ever-
increasing output.[37] The obsession with production results in 'an
implacable tendency to provide an opulent supply of some things
and a niggardly yield of others'.[38] He observed that a chronic
imbalance between private goods and public goods has existed in
New York City since the end of the Second World War. Old and
overcrowded schools, insufficient parks and playgrounds, dirty
streets, an overpaid and depleted police force, polluted air, a
public cleansing service short of men and equipment, unhealthy,
dirty and overcrowded local transport; all these shortcomings
still disfigure New York City today.

The ever-increasing proliferation of commercially produced
goods proceeds alongside this public poverty. The excessive
quantity of commercially produced and privately consumed goods
is, indeed, the cause of the shortage in the supply of public goods.
But, whatever the cause, the result is social discomfort and social
ill health.[39]

The misallocation of public resources within the available
global sum has also been criticised by economists of the liberal
school. Professor Harry Johnson, for example, contends that
resources are over-allocated to activities which appeal to a vague
but high-sounding national purpose, such as defence or research
and investment in established national industries; while there is
under-allocation to public amenities, social services, and the relief

of poverty, because here the social return is uncertain and vague, while the citizen is aware that his taxes will benefit other people.[40] Neither the government nor the governed appear to have inquired just who would benefit from the vast sums spent on Concorde apart from the thousands of highly paid workers employed on the job.

The affluent society is marked by a spirit of competition, not only among producers and distributors but also among consumers who vie with one another in keeping up with the Joneses.[41] The general tendency is towards the increase of inequality, stimulated partly by the desire of individuals to forge ahead of others, and partly by the restriction of the social services which are a major influence in promoting equality.

The contrast between private affluence and public squalor that one sees in New York does not exist in Britain to the same degree, partly because there is much less affluence and relatively more public expenditure. But the seeds of conflict are there. Mr (now Lord) George Brown refers in his autobiography to the difficulty facing any Labour government that wants to rebuild the country. It must provide more and better schools, colleges, hospitals, houses, roads, etc., which the voters themselves want. To finance its programme the government must impose high taxation. In his tour before the 1970 election, George Brown found that the very people who were most vociferously demanding improvements in the public services were those who were most angry about paying taxes.[42]

A similar situation exists in Sweden, despite – or perhaps because of – the far greater affluence attained there. The Social Democratic Party, which has governed the country for more than forty years, has tried to educate the electorate to understand and accept that they cannot have increased public services, particularly those requiring heavy capital investment, and also increase their private consumption equally fast without lapsing into inflation. The man in the street everywhere expects more and better services without paying for them by restricting his own purchasing power. The Swedish Social Democratic Party has had only limited success in getting people to understand that they must choose and cannot get a great deal for nothing.[43]

The view has been expressed by Professor Marshall that the welfare state cannot become a consumers' society in the manner of the affluent society because it must consider the satisfaction of genuine needs, the notion of fair shares, and give great attention to public services, the environment and other collectively provided goods.[44]

Signs of revolt can be discerned among young people, especially students, against the so-called consumers' society. This revolt is by no means confined to Britain, nor is it to be identified with the hippies and yippies, or that nebulous group known as the New Left, though they may have some beliefs in common. The movement is a revolt against the kind of affluent society which has emerged from the drive for ever-increasing production by commercial companies. It is a protest against a standard of values rather than a rejection of any specific level of material comfort. It stems from the conviction that an obsession with consumption, in the form it has assumed in the affluent society, is concerned only with the acquisition and spending of income or capital, not with its justification in terms of productive labour or service to the community. An illustration of this is that windfalls of any kind, whether the result of speculation, gambling, capital gains, inflated expense accounts, premium bonds, sweepstakes or other chances, are eagerly sought and welcomed, as though the concept of genuine earning had no moral basis whatever.

One critic suggests that virtues tend to become lost in a society geared to high consumption; and that to become, and to remain, a first-class people we must control, not be controlled by, the affluence we create.[45]

What 'control' of affluence involves is a question to which many different answers could be given. A more immediate question is the effect on our society of the relatively moderate degree of affluence we have so far achieved. A careful investigation carried out in three factories in Luton showed that while affluent manual workers enjoyed a standard of living comparable to that of many white-collar families, social integration had not taken place. The material basis of their lives might be similar to that of middle-class households, but the weekly wage earners had not undergone the much publicised process of *embourgeoisement*; nor had affluence stimulated within them a desire to be accepted by the new social milieu which surrounded them and thereby to acquire a higher status in society.[46] In short, class divisions had not been broken down although the unskilled or semi-skilled industrial workers had broken away from the working-class communities to which they formerly belonged. The middle-class workers of Mark Abrams, the workers whom Crosland described as having a middle-class psychology, and Lipset's aspiring workers who 'identify with the upper strata', failed to appear in the investigation.[47] What did emerge was a convergence in the attitudes and outlook of the working-class and white-collar groups during the post-war period. Both groups accepted trade union action as a means of protecting and improving their standard of living, and both groups regarded the nuclear family as a central life interest. These points of similarity in the outlook and life-styles of the manual and white-collar categories were described by the investigators as 'instrumental collectivism' and 'family-centredness'.[48]

The results are not encouraging as indications of progress towards a welfare society. Instrumental collectivism in this context means no more than using trade union activity as a method of securing higher personal gain. It contrasts with the collectivism which provides new or extended public services for the community at large or for those members of it with special needs. It also contrasts with the collectivism which has produced the consumers' co-operative movement. Family-centredness strikes a chilly reminder of indifference towards the underprivileged and the suffering, apathy towards collective goods, a narrow vision of the family group as a self-contained unit intent on securing its own comfort without much regard to the welfare of the larger community. The failure of affluence to overcome class divisions or class conflicts in our society gives no ground for satisfaction.

The family-centred life-style mentioned above is largely due to the great improvement which has taken place in the homes of the more affluent workers. Most family homes are more spacious, better furnished and equipped, and therefore more attractive to the better paid working man than they were formerly. He spends less of his time in the pub discussing the affairs of the world with his mates or pals, and more of his leisure watching television, decorating the house, driving and cleaning the car, and similar occupations.[49]

A report from Washington DC in 1970 stated that a high proportion of young British research and development scientists who had gone to the United States now wanted to return home. A long-term factor helping to reverse the brain drain was 'disenchantment with the emphasis on materialism in American life'. Other influences mentioned were the rising level of crime and the rapid deterioration of American cities[50] – all of them partly due to insufficient allocation of resources to public services.

In the Soviet Union a frank discussion took place in the press a few years ago on the discontent which can result from the so-called 'revolution of rising expectations'. The fear was expressed that as the USSR moves towards a greater abundance, the result may be more dissatisfaction, more complaints and grievances, due to 'hunger from surfeit', judging by the experiences of western countries.[51] In China, Chairman Mao Tse-Tung is said to be opposed to the pursuit of affluence, which he regards as corrupting.

Gambling throws some interesting sidelights on the questions of both affluence and equality. It appears from general observation that the amount of gambling increases with the rise of affluence. It might be argued that this is merely because those who gamble have a larger amount of money to spare for this activity. A different view was expressed in a government report which stated that the great rise in gambling in recent decades was due to 'a basic discontent in spite of the benefits of the affluent society'.[52]

The policies of the United Kingdom in this field are unusual in at least two respects. We have more legalised forms of gambling than any other country. We are also unique in the extent to which we permit private capital to encourage gambling and to profit from it. In most countries gambling is not entrusted to private enterprise, and in many of them state control discourages excessive growth.

The extent of gambling is estimated with great caution in the 1972 report of the Churches' Council on Gambling prepared by the Reverend Gordon E. Moody although most of the statistical data are speculative. He draws a distinction between the compulsive gamblers who are addicted to the activity, and the vast majority who simply enjoy the interest and uncertainty of the various forms of gambling. He estimates that about 725,000 thorough-going gamblers use the 14,500 betting offices which are to be found throughout the United Kingdom (a larger number of offices or shops than any other organisation, public or private). Adding the serious gamblers attending dog races, horse races, bingo halls and gaming clubs, he arrives at a total of about 1,300,000 'regular and committed gamblers' out of a vastly greater number who participate in these activities. These regular and committed gamblers are not engaged in a flutter, or a romantic adventure. 'For them gambling is life.' It replaces work and the normal ambitions and goals. It fulfils an essential need. Every individual in this category is in danger of slipping down into the abyss where all control is lost, and the journey ends in a ruined life. Mr Moody believes that the number of hard-core and compulsive gamblers has at least doubled in the past ten years.[53]

Whatever may be the causes of the attraction which gambling exerts over so many men and women of all ages, occupations, education, income and social background, most gamblers obviously do not believe in equality, since gambling is a means of creating or increasing inequality. Nor do the regular and committed gamblers believe in the dignity of work. Finally, the compulsive gambler, like the drug addict and the alcoholic, seeks an escape from reality. Hence it may be said that serious gambling is an indication of the failure of either the affluent society or the welfare state to provide well-being and fulfilment to a substantial number of its members. Compulsive gamblers should have no place in a welfare society.

What strikes one forcibly about the discussions concerning equality are (1) that the contentions put forward by the protagonists of conflicting views are usually *a priori* statements not based on any evidence, and (2) that the statements made by the proponents and opponents never really meet.

The opponents of equality usually base their arguments on a belief in freedom, which they assert it would be impossible to preserve in an egalitarian society. Professor Hayek, for example, argues against any attempt by the welfare state to introduce social justice in the distribution of goods on the ground that this requires discrimination between different people and their unequal treatment which is incompatible with a free society.[54] Freedom, he contends, is critically threatened by the governmental use of powers to promote economic equality.[55] Mr Samuel Brittan accepts with certain reservations the view that it is impossible to be an egalitarian liberal or a liberal egalitarian.[56]

Another argument put forward by liberals and conservatives who oppose equality is that competition and rivalry are the chief forces for promoting economic growth and raising living standards, and that competition inevitably produces unequal rewards. Thus they regard class distinctions and economic inequalities as the price to be paid for high productive efficiency.[57]

The opposing camp denounces this argument as a myth and argues that class barriers lead to economic and social stagnation as relations between classes become increasingly hostile. The proponents of equality tend to be mainly or exclusively concerned with those at the bottom of the ladder, who are in danger of being elbowed out and isolated from the mainstream of society. They are the champions of those poorly endowed by nature, the unskilled, the physically and mentally handicapped, the drop-outs from school and college, the victims of misfortune, the offspring of unhappy or broken homes, the low-paid workers in declining industries, the individuals with abnormally low energy or ability, those who find it hard to adjust to the requirements of modern industry. The great and fundamental differences in natural ability which exist must not, they contend, be allowed to determine an individual's chances in life. These differences, whether physical or mental, can never be eliminated but their effect can be reduced by a sympathetic social policy which seeks to restore the balance between them and the more favoured members of society.[58]

This approach is negative in the sense that it aims at reducing disadvantages which handicap the underprivileged. It does not inquire whether differences in ability should or should not influence an individual's chances in life and his remuneration; and if they should not, what results might follow. *Towards Equality*, for example, does not ask what part the aggressive instincts play in creating or increasing inequality, and whether aggressive behaviour in economic life does or does not benefit the community. There are many personal characteristics, as well as social factors, which can create, maintain, increase or reduce equality in economic life. They include the personal qualities of drive, ambition, apathy, enthusiasm, laziness, industriousness, instability and infirmity of purpose. There are also many class and institutional influences.

The Alva Myrdal Report insists that greater equality in living conditions is a movement towards greater freedom, in which freedom from class divisions, insecurity, and the pressure of external circumstances will open the way to new and better human relationships based more on co-operation and community and less on self-assertion, competition, and conflict between groups. Equalising the conditions of life is seen as a way of changing human relations, of improving the social climate. If various groups of underdogs are unable to contribute to the common good, as they are in the present state of society, it cannot be argued that the policy of equality will harm the economy by slowing down growth and reducing efficiency.[59] This concept of freedom clearly has nothing in common with the liberty which Hayek thinks would be threatened by any state policy of redistribution or discrimination based on social justice.

Despite the arguments for greater equality in Sweden contained in the Alva Myrdal Report, recent events in that country reveal the strength of the opposition to attempts to achieve it. The Social Democratic Party, led by Mr Olof Palme, the new Prime Minister, came to power in 1970 pledged to a policy of creating greater social and economic equality by means of heavier taxes on the middle and upper classes and reform of the educational system in order to make university education and white-collar careers more easily available to young people from working-class homes. The election had taken place at a time of severe inflation with steeply rising prices for the necessities of life, and substantial unemployment among young graduates. In 1971 there occurred a series of strikes by teachers, judges, civil servants, university professors, municipal officers and other middle-class employees in support of wage increases which would have restored their differentials over the blue-collar workers. About 50,000 middle-class workers were involved in strikes or lockouts at this period, including 3,000 army officers. A Swedish publicist declared that it was a class struggle 'with academics and civil servants seeing the lower classes creeping up on them and not liking it at all; they see the state as being unsympathetic; its an impossible situation'. He disapproved of the strike by well-paid government employees who had only recently been granted the right to strike for he thought this was 'against the whole concept of our society'. Nonetheless the parameters of the situation were determined by a strongly held conviction, reinforced by a long tradition, that university-trained men and women with professional skills have a right to the status and monetary rewards which they had hitherto enjoyed compared with those who had less education and more easily acquired skills.

The opening up of secondary and higher education in Sweden began in 1962; but the effect had not been to make the university-educated middle income employees more egalitarian in their attitude towards the working class. It had made them more powerful numerically and more militant in defence of their advantageous position.

Both the proponents and opponents of equality agree in regarding income as a means of consumer enjoyment. Bertrand de Jouvenel points out that socialism was formerly 'an ethereal social doctrine' which aimed to achieve a good society in which human relations would be better than they now are, and more kindly feelings would prevail between man and man. This aspiration, he thinks, seems to have largely disappeared from contemporary reform movements. 'Redistribution takes its cue wholly from the society it seeks to reform.'[60] Consumerism is in control and material values reign supreme, particularly among the more militant groups of the New Left, who believe they are most drastically opposed to the existing state of society. But this allegation is not wholly true, for the leaders of the Swedish Social Democratic Party are conscious of the need for much wider and deeper changes in human relations than the equalisation of consumer demand. Michael Young has also argued that we suffer from the mono-culture of capitalism and that a pluralistic value system would help to establish a greater degree of equality in society, for it would place a lower value on money and economic power, and more on other values.[61]

There is a substantial measure of general agreement in Britain about reducing inequalities in regard to certain categories such as women, retired pensioners, slum-dwellers and the homeless, the sick, handicapped persons, unemployed, students, one-parent families, etc., by providing on an increased scale various kinds of assistance for them in cash and in kind. There is agreement that equality of opportunity should be promoted by state-assisted university education, vocational training and guidance, and similar measures. There is agreement that family responsibilities should be taken into account – up to a point. There is agreement that taxation should be progressive – up to a point. Beyond that there is little or no agreement and the choice of direction must ultimately rest on value-preferences, which each person will choose for himself. The choice will often be influenced by personal circumstances. Whatever choice is made, the value selected will usually be 'supported' by a number of arguments based on untested statements and usually unprovable assumptions. The discussants seldom, if ever, recognise that while it is possible to have an unjustly unequal society, it is also possible to have a justly unequal society and an unjustly equal society. It may be admitted that this would depend on what one understands by justice; but most people would agree that there is an essential difference between an inherited fortune, a fortune acquired by property speculation or gambling, and a fortune acquired by exceptional ability as a film-star, an author, a surgeon, an opera-singer, an inventor, an industrialist, an exporter or a retailer.

In his great book on equality, Richard Tawney remarked that those who defend inequality as essential to the preservation of freedom are always thinking only of the powers of government, whereas the real threat to freedom in the contemporary state lies in the economic sphere, where giant commercial corporations exercise immense uncontrolled powers over the lives of their employees. Political arrangements may be adequate to restrain excesses or abuse of governmental power, yet economic conditions may allow or encourage them, so that a society can be at one and the same time politically free and economically unfree. 'It may be protected against arbitrary action by the agents of government, and be without the security against economic oppression which corresponds to civil liberty.'[62]

If liberty and equality conflict, Tawney held that liberty is to be preferred but he believed that this would seldom occur.[63] He rejected as an unproved dogma the economists' argument that the diminution of inequality would result in the discouragement of enterprise and the depletion of capital,[64] and suggested that a lower average income with greater equality might produce a happier society than one with a higher average income distributed with greater inequality[65] – this too being an unproved assumption. Tawney conceived equality as involving 'the prevention of sensational extremes of wealth and power by public action for the public good'[66] – a very moderate statement. He considered the chief instruments for achieving these ends to be progressive taxation and the provision of a greatly expanded programme of social services. We now know that the problem is far more complex and the solutions far more diverse.

An important recent contribution to the debate on equality is W. G. Runciman's study, *Relative Deprivation and Social Justice*. In this he separates the question whether inequalities are legitimate by the standard of social justice from the question whether they ought in fact to be redressed.[67] Socialists frequently speak and write as though equality were an absolute good overriding all other goods. This he refutes by remarking that equality can in some circumstances have evil effects by upgrading vicious or evil or unsocial elements in society and downgrading constructive elements. It could possibly reduce the efforts of the most creative individuals and reduce the productivity of the nation. The same is true of other goods. Justice, Runciman declares, is not a sole and overriding good, and few modern writers on justice would claim that it is. 'But justice is nonetheless a good which in the absence of stronger obligations ought *prima facie* to be put into effect. . . .'[68]

At last we are beginning to see some common sense on this question. Runciman insists that the change to a socially just society could not be either quick or painless, and any immediate reform might be incompatible with utilitarian criteria of welfare. Therefore it does not necessarily follow from the fact that society is not just that social justice should be done. To make twentieth-century Britain socially just might, perhaps, 'reduce its efficiency and diminish the satisfactions of some people more than it augmented the happiness of others.'[69] Here he is implying that one cannot ignore the historical development of a country in deciding whether drastic change is feasible at any given time.

What emerges from this discussion is that the principle of diminishing returns can and should be applied in the realm of ideas and public policies. This principle is one of the old so-called 'laws' of economics, and it can also be applied to social and political concepts. Thus, the concept of reducing inequality or achieving greater equality is valuable up to a point; but thereafter its value is likely to decline more and more rapidly. This notion does not imply that we can predict at what point the application of the concept of equality will yield diminishing returns.

Until recently discussion on equality tended to concentrate on questions of earnings or wealth and to neglect other kinds of inequality, such as the possession of industrial or commercial power. There have been occasional reminders of the terrible effects on the lives of the workpeople when a factory is closed or a take-over plays havoc with established expectations of employment and disrupts good industrial relations. The sit-in at the Upper Clyde shipyard and the work-in at the Triumph motor-cycle factory were spontaneous attempts to rectify, or at least contest, the immense inequalities of power in modern industry. Britain has been backward in giving the workpeople's representatives a place on the board of directors; and a frequent practice in the take-over of one firm by another is to omit genuine consultation with trade unions or consideration of the employees' point of view, and to go no further than a statement that their interests will be taken into account.

If we are to move more closely towards a welfare society, we must secure a reduction in the vast inequalities which still exist in the economic, social and cultural spheres. We must enlarge the scope of the discussion and try to widen the area over which there is a consensus of view. We must avoid presenting the argument in terms which imply that soaking the rich is the main or sole objective; and envy, greed and jealousy the principal motives. We must emphasise that if social justice is to be a major criterion in determining the distribution of wealth and incomes, *laissez-faire* collective bargaining is incompatible with that criterion, and that market forces and relative bargaining strength are no more influenced by considerations of social justice in determining wage rates for the various categories of labour than they are in determining incomes from property or land values. A welfare society would therefore have to accept some better means of dividing the cake. In other words, there should be an incomes policy, whether it is controlled by the government, or by an independent body, or by a joint organ comprising the government, the Trades Union Congress and the Confederation of British Industry, or some other representative body.

Economic and social equality can never be substantially attained in a modern industrial state, whether it has a capitalist, communist[70] or a mixed economy. Moreover no one has ever lived in a truly egalitarian society, so no one knows if they or others would enjoy life in such a society. To dislike some of the inequalities which disfigure our present society does not mean we should like or be prepared to accept a high degree of social and economic equality. It is unlikely that a substantial proportion of the British nation would wish to live in such a state. Indeed, some of the most fervent advocates of an egalitarian society enjoy a personal standard of living far higher than what would be possible if greater equality were brought about.

The only conclusions which can safely be drawn are that rather less inequality at both ends of the scale would probably result in an overall increase in national welfare; and that the welfare state and the welfare society must learn from empirical experience what degree of social and economic equality or inequality results in the optimum amount of welfare for the community as a whole. *A priori* judgements and doctrinaire statements on the subject are to be profoundly distrusted.

Finally, a few words about methods. Some progress at the bottom end of the scale could be made by raising the incomes of the lowest paid workers by means of a national minimum wage, or by an extension of wage councils or similar bodies, or by a change of outlook and machinery in regard to the determination of wages and salaries. Other changes in distribution at the higher levels could be brought about by replacing estate duty by a progressive lifetime capital receipts tax, and treating capital gains in the same way as income for purposes of taxation.[71] A tax credit scheme also could have beneficial advantages for the lowest income groups.

In a welfare society, however, the collectively provided services, including not only education, health, housing and social security, but also environmental goods such as parks and playgrounds, publicly supported arts and entertainments, good physical planning and civic design, should be regarded as income in kind, and therefore as forming part of everyone's standard of life just as much as the spending money in their pockets or bank accounts. The more these are increased and improved, the more will the egalitarian aspects of our society be advanced.

In order to bring about such an increase or improvement we need not rely exclusively on allocating larger resources from the public revenue derived from taxation, as we have in the past. Much could be done by means of personal service. As Professor Dahrendorf pointed out in his Reith Lectures, 'we need people to do the things which we need in order to improve our lives and increase our life-chances. This may well be a task to which everybody in a mature society should make a personal contribution; a contribution of time, not of money. Why should we not ask every citizen to devote one year of his or her life to public service?'[72] He was careful to explain he was not thinking of anything resembling military conscription for the young but of a flexible obligation which could be fulfilled at different times in the lives of different people, not necessarily always in a single period, and with a choice as to the kind of service each individual would prefer to render.

This proposal is one which I would applaud not only as a method of helping to improve the social services and the quality of life; but also as a means of recognising at long last that the citizen has duties as well as rights. It would also show that a welfare state cannot rely only on what the government does, but must also depend on the efforts, the attitudes and the values of the citizens who form the welfare society.

NOTES

1   Alva Myrdal, 'Report to the Swedish Social Democratic Party', *Towards Equality* (1971).
2   *Socialism in the New Society* (1962), p. 4.
3   ibid., pp. 5–7. Bernard Shaw advocated complete equality in *The Intelligent Woman's Guide to Socialism and Capitalism* (1928), *passim*.
4   ibid., p. 11.
5   ibid., p. 16.
6   ibid., p. 21.
7   See p. 23.
8   'Whose Welfare State', in *Conviction*, Norman Mackenzie (ed.) (1958), pp. 55–6, 63.
9   Bernard Crick and William A. Robson (ed.), *Taxation Policy*. See especially the essays on 'Poverty and Taxation' by D. Piachaud, 'The Reform of Wealth Taxes in Britain' by A. A. Akinson and 'Death Duties' by Cedric Sandford.
10 G. Tegner, *Social Security in Sweden* (1956), p. 15.
11 Richard M. Titmuss, *Essays on the Welfare State* (1958), p. 31.
12 'The Long-Term Planning of Taxation', in Crick and Robson, op. cit., p. 165.
13 Alva Myrdal Report, *Towards Equality*, pp. 106–7.
14 J. E. Meade, *The Inheritance of Inequalities: Some Biological, Demographic, Social and Economic Factors*, Third Keynes Lecture in Economics, Proceedings of the British Academy, Vol. 59 (1973).
15 *Political Quarterly*, Vol. 45 (1974), p. 23.
16 Kurt Sontheimer and Wilhelm Bleek, *The Government and Politics of East Germany* (1975), p. 41.
17 ibid., p. 153.
18 B. de Jouvenel, *The Ethics of Redistribution* (1951), p. 70.

19 See Maurice Preston, 'Incentives, Distortion, and the System of Taxation', and Sir Richard Clarke, 'The Long-Term Planning of Taxation' in Crick and Robson (eds.), op. cit.
20 De Jouvenel, op. cit., p. 52.
21 ibid., pp. 62–3.
22 R. E. Money-Kyrle, *Psychoanalysis and Politics* (1951), pp. 121–2.
23 T. H. Marshall, *Sociology at the Cross Roads* (1963), pp. 254, 259.
24 B. Seebohm Rowntree, *Poverty, A Study of Town Life* (1901).
25 'Poverty as Relative Deprivation: Resources and Style of Living' in *Poverty, Inequality and Class Structure*, Dorothy Wedderburn (ed.) (1974), p. 15.
26 A. B. Atkinson, 'Poverty and Income Inequality in Britain' in Wedderburn (ed.), op. cit., pp. 58, 68; Frank Field, 'The New Poor: A Statistical Analysis' in *The New Poor*, Ian Henderson (ed.) (1973), pp. 52–731.
27 J. C. Kincaid, *Poverty and Equality in Britain* (1973) pp. 246–7; Ralph Miliband, 'Politics and Poverty', in Wedderburn (ed.) op. cit., pp. 183–94.
28 First Report from the Select Committee on Nationalised Industries 1967–8, Ministerial Control. BPP 371–1, Vol. 1, pp. 72–3.
29 ibid.
30 Barbara Wootton, *Remuneration in Welfare State*, Eleanor Rathbone Memorial Lecture (1961), p. 7.
31 ibid.
32 ibid., p. 10; The Social Foundations of Wage Policy (1953) *passim*.
33 Sir Geoffrey Vickers, 'Changing Ethics of Distribution', *Futures* (June 1971), pp. 117 et seq.
34 ibid., pp. 131–2.
35 W. Arthur Lewis, *Socialism and Economic Growth* (1971), pp. 7–8.
36 Marshall, op. cit., p. 318.
37 J. K. Galbraith, *The Affluent Society* (1971), p. 252.
38 ibid., p. 12.
39 ibid., p. 253.
40 'The Economic Approach to Social Questions', *Economica*, Vol. 137 (February 1968).
41 ibid., pp. 2, 124.
42 George Brown, *In my Way* (1971), p. 271.
43 Gunnar Myrdal, 'The Place of Values in Social Policy', *Journal of Social Policy* (Jan. 1972).
44 op. cit., p. 284.
45 Pauline Gregg, *The Welfare State* (1967), p. 312.
46 John H. Goldthorpe et al., *The Affluent Worker: Political Attitudes and Behaviour* (1968), p. 79.
47 John H. Goldthorpe et al., *The Affluent Worker in the Class Structure* (1969), pp. 144–5.
48 ibid., p. 27.
49 Peter Willmott, 'The Influence of Some Social Trends upon Regional Planning', p. 10. A paper presented to a joint conference of the Social Science Research Council and the Centre for Environmental Studies (5–7 July 1968).
50 *The Times* (23 March 1970).

51 'Russian Doubts on Affluent Society', *The Times* (10 February 1968).
52 'Discontents of an Affluent Society', *The Times* (19 December 1962).
53 Gordon E. Moody, *The Facts about the 'Money Factories'* (1972), (The Churches Council on Gambling, 1972), pp. 7–8, 62–3.
54 F. A. Hayek, *The Constitution of Liberty* (1960), pp. 259–60.
55 ibid., pp. 289–90.
56 Samuel Brittan, *Capitalism and the Permissive Society,* pp. 124–35.
57 Alva Myrdal Report, *Towards Equality,* p. 18.
58 ibid., p. 17.
59 ibid., p. 15.
60 De Jouvenel, op. cit., p. 43.
61 'Is Equality a Dream?', Rita Hinden Memorial Lecture (1972), p. 7.
62 R. H. Tawney, *Equality* (1931), p. 243.
63 ibid., pp. 238–9.
64 ibid., p. 213.
65 ibid., p. 168.
66 ibid., p. 238.
67 W. G. Runciman, *Relative Deprivation and Social Justice* (1966), p. 292.
68 ibid., p. 253.
69 ibid., pp. 288–9.
70 One of the curious aspects of contemporary discussion in Britain about incomes and prices is that no reference is made to the situation in the communist countries of Eastern Europe or Yugoslavia. In the German Democratic Republic, for example, remuneration is based on the principle of 'to each according to his ability, to each according to his achievement'–not, as Marx proposed, according to his need. Those who believe that the abolition of capitalism and the introduction of a communist regime would result in economic equality, would be surprised and possibly disappointed at the degree of inequality which exists in the GDR and Eastern Europe.
71 These changes are discussed in A. B. Atkinson, *Unequal Shares* (1972), pp. 251–5; and 'Death Duties' by Cedric Sandford in Crick and Robson (eds), op. cit.
72 *The Listener* (2 January 1975), p. 7.

Chapter V

Human Values
in the Welfare State

During the past thirty years the British people have been obsessed by two basic aims: the demand for equality and the desire for economic growth. These two objectives were not always voiced by the same people. The demand for equality has been put forward continually in one form or another by the Labour Party, the New Left, and trade union leaders when dealing with matters other than their own wage claims or collective bargaining; while the need for economic growth has been urged by all three political parties, by the Press and television, and by both sides of industry. Preoccupation with these aims has obscured some of the most profound features of contemporary society and led to the neglect of some essential needs. In this chapter I shall examine some of those neglected needs.

Let us begin by considering stability and change. For the first time in history change has become an end in itself. The rate of change and the scope of change are unprecedented. Changes in dress, hairstyle, manners, morals, relationships between parents and children and between the sexes, attitudes to obscenity and pornography, drug taking, the acquisition or possession of material goods, the authority of government, the right to work, housing, race relations, crime, the role of students, citizens' rights – all have changed more drastically and rapidly than in any previous time. Changes in such matters are often sought and adopted as something to be welcomed for their own sake without questioning their intrinsic merit. Part of this continuous flux is due to the marketing and advertising policies of commercial firms who, in order to dispose of their output, direct their efforts to making people dissatisfied with what they already have or persuading them that they would be more satisfied with the latest product. This applies particularly to dress, motorcars and other commodities subject to annual changes of fashion. The continual mounting of costly advertising campaigns designed by astute specialists skilled in the art of influencing human desires has the effect which even a fervent believer in market forces concedes 'causes some people to be more dissatisfied with their lot than they otherwise would be',[1] A more important result of commercial advertising is that it stimulates the demand for consumer goods compared with collectively provided goods and services.

The great increase in the rate of change is, however, by no means confined to goods and services sold in the market. The physical environment, institutions of all kinds, and many aspects of our culture, are subject to accelerating rates of change which often involve sharp breaks with even the recent past. It has been, and still is, widely assumed that change is both desirable and inevitable, and that people must adjust to change rather than that change must be controlled. Sir Geoffrey Vickers has questioned these assumptions in a penetrating book. The word 'change', he writes, is in everyone's mouth and the word 'instability' is seldom heard. 'Yet instability, not change, is the challenge of our time; stability not "changelessness" is its primary need. It is essential to distinguish these two ideas, change and instability; for though they overlap, they are radically different.'[2] Stability is not the enemy of change but the condition of lasting and acceptable change. Nor is stability to be confused with the static, the static with the stagnant, and the stagnant with putrifying.[3]

The accelerating rate of change in so many different spheres has made it difficult for many people to make sufficiently rapid adjustments to the changes. It is not fanciful to believe that some of the increased drug addiction, alcoholism, hooliganism, violence, and deviant behaviour among the young can be ascribed to inability to adjust to current rates of change.[4]

The clearest indication that assumptions about the desirability and inevitability of change are being questioned is the resistance shown recently to plans for physical development which would obliterate familiar scenes and replace existing landmarks and habitations by new and unfamiliar forms of urban technology. Examples are rejection of the Greater London Council's plans for redevelopment of Covent Garden, the outcry at Westminster City Council's first plan for Piccadilly Circus, and the strong opposition which killed the so-called motorbox which would have transformed vast areas of inner London to provide motorways.

It seems obvious that a welfare society would try to achieve a greater degree of stability than we now enjoy; that this would involve a less uncritical acceptance of change than is often manifested; and that the advantages of such a revaluation might yield both individual and social benefits.

A remarkable fact is that in Britain we have made no attempt whatever to teach, or even to formulate, a political philosophy appropriate to the welfare state. We have devised and applied policies of many different kinds by central and local government in order to promote the welfare of particular categories of persons or of the entire nation. We have conferred rights to welfare of various kinds: to free education, to medical treatment, to supplementary benefits, to social security benefits, to subsidised council housing, to legal aid, to assistance for the disabled and to welfare benefits of many other types, and the government is pledged to avoid mass unemployment. But we have not formulated, far less tried to apply, any body of obligations related to these rights. The emphasis has rested exclusively on rights, to the total exclusion of duties. The result is an intellectual and moral vacuum which has been filled by discord, violence, clamour, militancy, conflict and endless demands for more money, shorter hours, longer holidays, additional or better social services – and more rights to everything for everybody. Even the qualities of fellowship and a sense of community which might have mitigated the selfishness and greed of our society have been conspicuous by their absence under both Labour and Conservative governments since 1945. The spirit of unity, altruism, self-sacrifice and comradeship which carried the nation through the Second World War has found no place in the welfare state, except in a few activities such as blood donation,[5] nursing and social work. Many doctors, nurses and some teachers set an example which is not widely followed in other vocations.

Sidney and Beatrice Webb were among the founders of the welfare state. Much of their great work was concerned with preventing destitution, expanding the scope and raising the standard of education, providing a health service, finding alternatives to capitalism or remedying its defects, abolishing the poor law, and other large issues of social reform. They were engaged, they said, in the task of cleaning up the base of society, but despite their immense efforts in devising and advocating measures of practical reform, the Webbs regarded the moral factor as the ultimate criterion of society. They did not deny that moral defects of character can cause destitution in some cases. They recognised that if there were moral and spiritual degradation; if a large part of the population were reduced to drinking, begging, cringing and lying; if the mass of each generation were submerged in 'coarseness and bestiality, apathy and cynical scepticism of every kind', then society was sick. They saw the ultimate object of every scheme of reform as the spiritual and moral improvement of human character and an advance in the standard of citizenship.[6] The Webbs' philosophy seems very far away from the climate of opinion which has prevailed in Britain in recent decades.

Whatever shortcomings from a libertarian point of view the communist countries display, they do not neglect to inculcate a social ethic which conforms with their political and economic regime and that is essential to its maintenance. In the German Democratic Republic, basic socialist rights which aim at integrating the individual into the social and political order lay a strong emphasis on complementary basic duties. Rights and duties are, indeed, inseparable in the GDR's legal theory. The right to work is buttressed by the corresponding duty to work, the right to be educated by the duty to accept the education.

Moreover, in the German Democratic Republic collaboration in shaping the process of production is not simply a right conferred on the worker of which he may avail himself or not, as he pleases. 'As a result of nationalisation', we are told in a recent study, 'he is not only employee and wage-earner, but also – as we should say – employer and owner. His rights therefore imply duties, arising out of his co-ownership of what is public property. Anyone who neglects his duties in the socialist production process, or who misuses his rights, does not offend against a contract with an employer, but harms common property and thereby injures his own interests. Those rights, which arise out of the fact of public property for each employee, are therefore identical with duties, the primary one being that of increased productivity.'[7]

A similar idea that the maximum fulfilment of the individual is to be found through his or her pursuit of the collective interest is one of the most potent elements in the new social ethic which is evolving in communist China.[8]

In Britain the nationalisation of basic industries and services has had no influence whatever on the demands and attitudes of the employees. There have been official strikes in the coal industry, on the railways, on the airlines and in the Post Office – all publicly owned; for the first time civil servants, teachers in the municipal schools, dustmen in the municipal cleansing departments, the staff of state hospitals, ambulance drivers and firemen, have all been on strike in recent years. These are all publicly owned and operated services in which no trace of capitalism or private ownership exists.

It is therefore clear that public ownership does not by itself introduce a different attitude towards work or a new social ethic which would give priority to the good of the community. An experienced industrial psychologist believes that nationalised industry has to face psychological problems of a similar nature to those of the privately owned firms, but whereas the large commercial companies have moved towards decentralisation, the public corporations have tended to move in the opposite direction.[9] Professor Hugh Clegg has expressed the opinion that the public corporation has not so far achieved relations with its staff which are any better than those prevailing under good employers in the private sectors.[10] The conclusion reached is that the Labour Party appears to have a quite unjustified faith in its ability to solve the human problems of the worker by eliminating the profit motive and private ownership of industry.[11]

Inter-union disputes have led to prolonged strikes in both the public and private sectors of industry. Examples are the conflicts between the NUR and ASLEF on the railways, SOGAT and NGA in the newspaper industry, and TGWU and AUEW in the motor industry. These bitter quarrels have been pursued with ruthless strikes in complete disregard of the danger of injuring a nationalised undertaking, bankrupting a national newspaper, or increasing the sale of foreign cars. The traditional image of trade unions defending the workers from exploitation by greedy capitalists has not the faintest relation to the contemporary situation.

It is generally recognised at home and abroad that industrial relations are in a chaotic and anarchic condition in many of Britain's largest industries, and that in this respect we are far behind other industrial nations, whether capitalist or communist. One contributory cause is the lack of any attempt to inculcate, or even to formulate, a work ethic on the part of parents, teachers, clergymen, politicians, statesmen, philosophers, writers or anyone else.

The weakness of the communist doctrine is that it is trying to suppress individual achievement and the satisfaction which it brings. In Marxist theory individual achievement should be absorbed within a collective work morality. Everywhere in East Germany 'a new, socialist morality is preached and practised, a morality intended to overcome the individualism of a bourgeois past and create new, collective forms of living in which "I" is to be absorbed into "we" '.[12] Such an attempt to suppress completely the egoistic self-centred side of life is likely to be both misguided and impossible. It will produce frustration and distress. The happiest individuals are those who have achieved a sound balance between the self-regarding and the other-regarding interests or activities of man in society. Hence the welfare state should aim at evolving a society in which the citizens can attain individual satisfaction and also contribute to collective or community welfare. In this respect the welfare state can be superior to the communist or fascist regime, in which the totalitarian state makes unlimited demands on the individual's loyalty, obligations and the suppression of personal desires. Indeed, for this very reason communism and fascism are incapable of creating a welfare society.

Almost the only axiom in the British welfare state concerning the workers as such has been the responsibility of the government to maintain full employment. Beyond this no government of any political party has ventured. But full employment is essentially a negative concept aimed at preventing heavy unemployment. It lacks any sense of purpose or direction. Its object is to ensure that all the workers will be busy all the time, making goods and providing services. It does not inquire what kinds of goods and services, or for what ends they are produced. 'Keeping everyone at work would have been inconceivable as a major objective to any society before our own', writes August Heckscher, 'and none of the utopias has suggested this to be an ideal condition. But it fits in with the basic assumptions of the welfare state: a people occupied, secure and healthy, without questions asked as to what they seek to accomplish or, for that matter, why they desire to go on living.'[13]

There are signs that perceptive observers are beginning to question the validity of the assumption that keeping busy and earning a good wage are the main if not the only essentials.

In a few factories pioneering attempts have been made to restore to the workers the pride they once possessed in the skill of their hands. In the Porsche motorcar factory in West Germany one man assembles and tests an entire engine. A similar exercise took place in the IBM computer works in France when a workman was allowed to assemble a substantial portion of a computer, which he tested and signed like an artist; it was, however, abandoned for technical reasons when integrated microcircuits were introduced.[14] Philips, the Dutch electronics firm, reduced the extreme division of labour among specialists in 1969, and entrusted the construction of a complete television set to only seven workers. Volvo and Saab-Scannia in Sweden have taken steps in the same direction. It is at least conceivable that an affluent welfare society could revive long-lost craft industries such as handcut glass or handmade bookbinding. India and China are both wise and farsighted in supporting and promoting the handcraft industries which preserve traditional skills and the satisfactions which those who work on the assembly line have never experienced.

The frustration of assembly-line workers, especially in motorcar manufacture, has become so widespread and acute that industrial leaders are at last realising that high rates of absenteeism, low quality of output, and chronically bad labour relations, are largely due to this cause. The monotony and fatigue, the so-called frenzy neurosis, of workers on the assembly line were all depicted by Charlie Chaplin in *Modern Times* forty years ago; but that was regarded as no more than a highly amusing film by the world's greatest comic-tragic actor. Now the Common Market Commissioner for Social Affairs has inaugurated a discussion with the International Labour Office on whether it is possible to find ways of prohibiting assembly-line work in the nine member countries.[15]

The alienation of the worker from his work has deep historical roots which must be understood if the malaise which afflicts our industrial society is to be cured. During the industrial revolution employers asserted that work was an unpleasant necessity which was performed only because of the fear of starvation. Thus work came to be regarded as the antithesis of all pleasure and happiness. In 'the dark Satanic mills' it was no longer performed for the master-craftsman in whose house the apprentice or the journeyman lived, or even to satisfy personal pride. It was performed merely for the sake of earning money in order to do other things. The worker was indoctrinated with an attitude that made him irresponsible, indifferent to the quality of his work, and unaware of whether or in what way it helped to satisfy social needs. So long as he was paid, he was indifferent to the type of work he was required to do. The employer, to an ever-increasing degree, took a similar view, so that as long as he could sell his goods, any question as to their usefulness was irrelevant.[16]

Modern research has identified powerlessness, futility, isolation and discontent as elements contributing to the alienation of the worker while freedom is regarded as its opposite. It is obvious that not all, or indeed not any, of these elements will exist in every work situation, and it would be absurd to suggest that all workers are alienated. A well-known investigation in four major industries in the United States brought to light the fundamental differences in printing, textiles, motorcar manufacture, and chemical production. In printing, as in other industries using craftsmen, manual skill still prevails, and the work involves discretion and initiative, both of which are essential to the dignity and self-respect of the worker. In continuous processes, such as those in automated oil refineries and heavy chemical plants, the operators do not work directly on the product nor is it even visible to them. Instead they monitor instruments which record what is happening or control the mechanism when it deviates from the norm. Here the employee must possess a high sense of responsibility and display initiative. But he is comparatively free to walk around the plant, to carry out his inspections not at absolutely fixed times, and within limits to exercise judgment.

The motorcar assembly line is the leading example of an industry in which the division of labour has been carried to its extreme point: traditional skills have been replaced by purely routine actions, and the workers are chained to the assembly line from which they cannot escape. They cannot display initiative, skill or responsibility. A similar position exists in modern textile mills, in which spinning or weaving is no longer carried out by skilled workers, and the operator's main task is to join together broken yarn. Manual skill, responsibility and discretion re-enter these automated or mechanised industries only through the workers who must install, maintain, repair and sometimes make the machines.[17]

That the alienation of workpeople is a major cause of industrial unrest, industrial conflict, and of apparently irrational disruption of an industry or a particular firm, is scarcely open to doubt. Behind the façade of indifference the workers may feel humiliated and hostile; given no responsibility they show none.[18]

Those who feel disposed to scoff at this diagnosis of our sick industrial relations should be asked to provide a convincing alternative explanation of total disregard of the interests of the economy, of their own industry, and even of their own firm, which has been displayed so often by workers mounting trade disputes involving stoppages of work in shipbuilding, the motorcar industry, the docks, coal mining and other vital industries. Again and again we have seen that discontented workers are deaf to appeals to the national interest.[19] We have already noted that nationalisation of an industry does not affect the attitude of the workers employed in it.

The senior executive in commerce, the director of an industrial company, the professional man in law or medicine, the scientist and the technologist, find it hard to understand the lot of the manual worker who regards his work mainly as a means of earning a living. To the former their work and careers are often the central life interest; and professionals, especially those engaged in teaching and research, or in medicine, spend much time attending conferences at home and abroad, visiting colleagues or institutions where interesting new work is in progress, and generally integrating their working life with their private life.[20] The semi-skilled or unskilled worker, on the other hand, gets little from his work except his pay: there is no significant job satisfaction. With increasing affluence he tends to become more home-orientated.[21]

A consequence of the greater importance of a family-centred life-style for the unskilled or semi-skilled worker is that his ambitions become focused on a rising standard of living, and especially on the acquisition of consumer durables – a washing machine, colour television, the car, etc. This in turn has made the level of wages more crucial than in the days of less affluence and more stable expectations; and the workers and their unions more moneyminded than in the past. No one who reads the newspapers or listens to the radio can fail to notice the continual harping on money, money, money (quite apart from the problem of inflation), which is a reflection of the phenomena discussed above.

It is not correct to lay the blame for the alienation of the worker from his work on the capitalist system because it can just as easily exist under a socialist or communist system of mass production – indeed, the problems can even be exacerbated if industrial disputes are forbidden and trade union action severely restricted, as they are in the communist countries of Eastern Europe. Moreover, capitalism caters more adequately for the consumption and leisure activities of the masses than any communist country has so far succeeded in doing, so to that extent it provides greater indirect reward from the production process, despite the alienation of the worker from his work.[22]

The alienation of the worker is partly due to his revolt against the authoritarian atmosphere of the factory, the steel mill and large-scale workplaces generally. The position in this respect is complex and influenced by conflicting trends. In the nineteenth and early twentieth centuries the authority of the employer or manager was generally accepted and seldom challenged. Its basis was the distinction between 'we' and 'them'. In recent decades increased affluence has made workers aware of the contrast between the opportunities for greater freedom in their private lives and the industrial discipline which restricts working relations. There has thus grown up a tension between leisure-time opportunities to create a meaningful existence and the demands on the worker to subordinate himself to the industrial process.[23] One consequence of this tension has been the powerful intervention of the shop steward as a mediating factor between management and work-people, so that in many factories it is virtually impossible for orders to be given unless they have been agreed by the shop stewards on behalf of the rank and file of the employees. Without the co-operation of the shop stewards it is today scarcely possible to maintain industrial disciplines.

It has recently been found that some forms of discipline which were regarded as essential are not necessary. An example is the belief that all employees in a factory or an office must work uniform hours to ensure efficiency. Hospitals and schools refused to contemplate recruiting qualified married women with young children who could only work part-time. It has now been shown that in many work situations the employees can be given a wide variety of choices in regard to the hours of starting and finishing work and its duration. The same applies to the length of holidays and extended leave of absence. Professor Galbraith presents the argument for abandoning wherever possible the notion that a standard week's work with uniform working hours is essential for the industrial system, even though to do so could cause some inconvenience. To insist on uniformity in all these matters is to make the needs of the industrial system our dominant concern rather than the freedom of the individual to shape his life in accordance with his personal wishes.[24]

It has been customary to consider more work or more leisure as alternatives which the employee could choose according to his preference after his basic needs have been met. Galbraith disputes the notion that industrial man will generally aim at less work and more leisure. He rejects the belief that work is intrinsically more unpleasant than non-work, for the opposite is often the case. Work-people will prefer leisure to work only if their interests are sufficiently cultivated to enable them to pursue leisure-time activities which yield genuine satisfaction, and provided they are sufficiently emancipated to rise above the siren voices which tell them to acquire more of everything in the shops if they want to be happy.[25] The American experience shows that the belief in a great expansion of leisure is a myth. Between 1941 and 1965 the average working week in US manufacturing rose from 40·6 to 41·1 hours and was still rising. From this trend Galbraith inferred that as incomes rise the workers will work longer hours and seek less leisure.[26] A similar position exists in Britain, where there is no evidence of the great increase in leisure time which is commonly believed to have occurred since the end of the Second World War. The belief is due to the decline in the length of the standard working week, but the actual hours worked in industry show little change during the past thirty or forty years. Clerical workers enjoy the shortest week, while executives and professionals not only work at least as long as manual workers on the average, but often much more of their time is filled with work.[27]

I doubt whether one can accept Professor Galbraith's conclusion that 'with more pleasant work and expanded wants, a man is somewhat more likely to choose more work than more leisure'.[28] Not long ago some Detroit car-workers stated that their purchasing needs were fully met by their earnings and they did not desire to earn more, but would follow leisure-time pursuits likely to give them greater pleasure rather than increased purchasing power.

There are, indeed, numerous cases on record of men giving up lucrative jobs in order to take up more enjoyable occupations. Among them is that of an aeronautical engineer in California following a teacher-training course; a US Navy Commander retiring in his mid-forties to become an episcopalian priest; a teacher in New York leaving to take a job as a real estate salesman; the general manager of the largest Volkswagen dealer joining the Peace Corps in his early forties at a fraction of his former salary.[29]

The late Karl Mannheim believed that the system of working primarily for profit and monetary reward is in process of disintegration. The masses are craving for a stable standard of living, but transcending that they want to feel that they are useful and important members of the community by virtue of what they contribute through their work.[30] I do not think the evidence supports the contention that reliance on earnings as a primary incentive is declining. On the contrary, the lack of other satisfactions in work, and the increased opportunities for enjoyment outside working life, have apparently accentuated the pursuit of monetary gain. Only if the workers were to become more integrated in their employment or more indoctrinated with a work ethic would the urge for increasing the financial rewards become less dominant.

Mannheim was on much firmer ground in asserting that the workpeople need to feel that they are performing a valuable social function which is recognised by others. It is possible that, by striking, the workers in a key industry can most effectively make others understand the significance of their work – the 'others' including employers, consumers and workers in the same or other industries.

A study of some highly sophisticated factories led to the suggestion that where the operation of a fully automated factory or oil refinery imposes a common discipline on management and the subordinates at all levels, the system of control is perceived as inherent in the production process rather than as an exercise in hierarchical authority imposed for its own sake by the management. In such a situation, the workpeople can more easily identify with the undertaking and they tend to become socially integrated with the enterprise.[31] A classic example of such a situation is a ship, where the crew do not normally think of a 'we' and 'you' attitude towards the captain and other officers. Another example is a hospital, where the interests of the patients justify the exercise of authority in a system of unique complexity.

It is difficult to reconcile the integrative function of technological complexity with the phenomenon that it is in the most highly mechanised, automated and sophisticated plants that management is most often challenged and its authority denied, and where loyalty to the enterprise seems to be conspicuously absent. Motorcar manufacture in Britain is the industry most frequently afflicted by stoppages of work, usually resulting from conflicts between the managers and the managed. Newspaper production and airline operation fall into the same category of highly complex undertakings equipped with advanced technology but subject to frequent disruption caused by labour disputes. The fact that in these types of industry it is most easy for a small minority of workers or a small unit in the enterprise to disrupt the whole undertaking does not explain why this disruption should occur if the integrating process is as strong as has been suggested by Goldthorpe and his colleagues. Nor is it easy to accept the view that in the most highly evolved types of enterprise the blue-collar worker is generally 'lukewarm to unions and loyal to his employer'.[32]

The modern factory manager, uncomfortably aware of the fact that his workpeople are not integrated, or at least not highly integrated, in their workplace, or are suffering from a sense of alienation, will offer alternative methods of gaining their loyalty and co-operation. These will include dances, outings, holiday centres, etc. Some of these fringe benefits are valuable, but they do not touch the unsatisfied psychological need of employees for responsibility, self respect, a sense of fulfilling a social purpose, pride in their work, and a worthwhile status.[33]

In the German Democratic Republic the anti-egalitarian conditions which have been introduced – or more precisely re-introduced – for economic reasons in the factories etc., are counteracted by making the undertaking the focal point of all social life, such as clubs, libraries, cultural centres, further education, housing associations for the workers, social insurance, holiday travel, children's camps, and discount shopping facilities at the workplace.[34] All this goes far beyond the limited range of activities comprised in the concept of staff welfare by British companies. The aim is clearly to create a sense of community among the workforce. In the West German Federal Republic some of the leading firms, such as the great chemical firm of Bayer, attempt to provide for all the needs of their employees from cradle to grave, including crèches, schools, old persons' homes, clinics, etc. The result appears to have succeeded at least to the extent that strikes are virtually unknown.

In Japan the employees feel a deep sense of loyalty to the enterprise and pride in its achievements; while the employer has a sense of genuine concern for the well-being of the workers. Two features of the Japanese relationship are unique. One is the general assumption that an employee will remain in the service of the same employer throughout his working life, unless various causes such as marriage in the case of women, resignation, dismissal for misconduct, or closing down of the firm, etc., end the relationship at an earlier point. This assumption of a permanent relationship is not confined to industry and commerce, but applies also to universities, hospitals and other types of employment.

The other feature of Japanese life is that the employee's personal affairs are not so remote from his working life as they are in the West. The owner or manager of a firm will be a highly honoured guest at the wedding of a member of his staff. A great many social entertainments for employees are organised and paid for by the firm. The men are entertained by Geisha girls, and their wives are not invited. This impoverishes family life but it helps to bind the employee to his firm. To dismiss the Japanese relationship as paternalism is superficial and misleading. It overlooks the fact that Japan is the only highly industrialised capitalist country in which there are so far no signs of class conflict. It is even possible to say that there are no clear class divisions but rather an elaborate status system.

Whatever the causes may be, the German Democratic Republic, the Federal Republic of West Germany, and Japan, all have systems of labour relations which are unquestionably better than that which exists in Britain. In all those countries the relations between management and workpeople are more peaceful and harmonious, productivity and economic growth are much higher, the countries are more prosperous, and the workers feel less alienated from their employment. What is lacking in many British firms, large and small, is not 'good management', or 'less bloody-mindedness' on the part of the workpeople or their unions, but a sense of community among all those who belong to the enterprise. It is this which is at present lacking, and until we can acquire it, a welfare society will not exist and the welfare state will have built its elaborate stucture on sand.

NOTES

1   Samuel Brittan, *Capitalism and the Permissive Society* (1973), p. 17.
2   *Freedom in a Rocking Boat: Changing Values in an Unstable Society* (1970), p. 121.
3   ibid., p. 128.
4   An American writer believes that the question is not whether the community is being subjected to too much innovation, but whether the innovation is of a kind which menaces the concept of community itself, whether we are going to have a culture which has meaningful values that can be handed down from one generation to the next. August Heckscher, *The Public Happiness* (1963), p. 26.
5   Richard M. Titmuss, *The Gift Relationship* (1970), *passim*.
6   Sidney and Beatrice Webb, *The Prevention of Destitution* (1911), p. 2 and ch. 10. See also my introduction to their *English Poor Law History*, Part I, *The Old Poor Law* (1911, reprinted 1963).
7   Kurt Sontheimer and Wilhelm Bleek, *The Government and Politics of East Germany* (1975), p. 107.
8   Derek Bryan, 'Changing Social Ethics in Contemporary China', *The Political Quarterly* (Jan.–March 1974), p. 55.
9   J. A. C. Brown, *Social Psychology of Industry* (1970), p. 302.
10 Hugh Clegg, *Industrial Democracy and Nationalisation* (1951), and *Labour Relations in London Transport* (1950).
11 Brown, op. cit., pp. 302–3.
12 Sontheimer and Bleek, op. cit., p. 106.
13 op. cit., p. 218.
14 Dennis Gabor, 'Fighting Existential Nausea' in *Technology and Human Values* (1966), p. 16.
15 Alan Osborn, 'EEC Fights Factory Boredom', *Daily Telegraph* (28 June 1973), p. 3.
16 Brown, op. cit., pp. 37–8.
17 Robert Blauner, *Alienation and Freedom* (1964), Chs 2, 7, and *passim*.
18 Brown, op. cit., p. 37.
19 'Trying to induce discontented workers to produce more by telling them of the serious economic plight of the country is like the action of a well-meaning teetotaller who hires the Albert Hall and lectures to a host of alcoholics on the evil effects of drinking to excess.' Brown, op. cit., p. 292.
20 Peter Willmott, 'The Influence of Some Social Trends upon Regional Planning', pp. 3–4. A paper presented to a joint conference of the Social

Science Research Council and the Centre for Environmental Studies (5–7 July 1968).

21 John H. Goldthorpe et al., *The Affluent Worker: Political Attitudes and Behaviour* (1968), p. 78.

22 Andre Gorz, 'Work and Consumption' in *Towards Socialism*, Perry Anderson and Robin Blackburn (eds) (1965), p. 349.

23 Alva Myrdal Report to the Swedish Social Democratic Party, *Towards Equality* (1971), p. 106.

24 J. K. Galbraith, *The New Industrial State* (1967), p. 367.

25 ibid., p. 365.

26 ibid., pp. 363–4.

27 Willmott, op. cit., p. 16.

28 op. cit., pp. 363–4.

29 Damon Stetson, 'Americans Take to the Two-Career Life', *The Times* (24 July 1968).

30 Karl Mannheim, *Diagnosis of our Time* (1943), pp. 13–14.

31 John H. Goldthorpe et al., *The Affluent Worker in the Class Structure* (1969), p. 4.

32 ibid., citing Blauner, *Alienation and Freedom*, pp. 181–2

33 Brown, op. cit., pp. 37–8.

34 Sontheimer and Bleek, op. cit., p. 109.

Chapter VI

Growth and the Environment

Economic growth is one of the commonest facts of history. The Industrial Revolution was not the beginning of economic growth but only a phase of it which saw the introduction of technological inventions which immensely speeded up the process and had significant social consequences. Economic growth had taken place for thousands of years before that in all save the most rigidly traditional societies. What is new in our own time is the intense preoccupation with economic growth which most countries have shown during the past thirty or forty years. I believe this is mainly due to the changed attitude towards poverty to which reference was made in Chapter II.[1]

Whatever the cause, the unquestionable fact is that we have become accustomed to regard the statistics of economic growth as the basic indication of whether a nation is moving forwards or backwards, not only absolutely but also in relation to other countries. We regard the so-called league table of comparative growth rates as no less authentic an indication of national form than the league table of football performance from which it gets its name.[2]

The obsession with economic growth is not a feature peculiar to the welfare state. It is found in virtually every state whatever its politico-economic regime and whatever its stage of development. But since welfare states share the widespread belief in economic growth, the relation of the former to the latter requires examination; and we must also consider the place of economic growth in a welfare society.

'The production of material goods, urgent or otherwise', remarked Professor Galbraith, 'is the accepted measure of our progress. Both this product and the means for increasing it are measurable and tangible.'[3] Any alternative calculus of human effort is far more difficult to quantify and lacks precision. The principal figure in determining growth is the Gross National Product

(GNP) but this can be buttressed by figures relating to imports and exports, capital formation, the balance of payments, and average per capita income. These are regarded as the basic criteria of economic well-being. They are eagerly scrutinised by politicians, civil servants, journalists, businessmen, financiers, economists and trade union leaders.

The method of compiling the Gross National Product is easy to criticise on the ground of what it excludes. It does not include the goods and services which people produce for their personal consumption or investment, or the vast amount of work which wives and mothers, and to an increasing extent husbands and fathers, perform in the home or in family-directed activities or in voluntary work outside the home. Nor are the non-monetary benefits which we receive in kind from public services such as health and education translated into monetary terms and included in the Gross National Product.[4] Economists and statisticians are fully aware of these limitations[5] but they have had little influence on the hypnotic effect which the figures of economic growth exert on public opinion.

The obsession with economic growth has been castigated by Galbraith as due to tradition and myth.[6] It is, however, possible to give a perfectly rational explanation of why important groups in our society are attached to the growth concept. Ministers and their officials see it as a method of increasing the revenue without raising taxes, a highly acceptable situation which enables a government to provide more or better services without seeming to take a higher proportion of personal or corporate income (though it may actually be doing so in a progressive fiscal system). Moreover, although economic growth by itself does not result in greater equality, it may serve as an alternative to redistribution by relieving some of the tensions and poverty arising from inequality.[7] Furthermore, faster growth may facilitate a more equal distribution of income and a more equal consumption by enabling an increase of public expenditure on social services to be financed out of taxation. It is easier, suggests Professor Beckerman, to improve the relative position of the lower income groups if this does not necessitate an absolute reduction in the standard of living of the better-off members of society.[8] This consideration can be of importance at a time when the problem of taxable limits has arisen in several European countries, including Britain.

There are also other aspects of the matter. Professor Sir Arthur Lewis points out that in some countries, such as Great Britain, the wage earners and their trade unions put forward demands at regular intervals for higher remuneration as well as for greater expenditure on the social services. If income per head does not grow, such demands can only be met at the expense of other groups, and this will lead to civil strife. Bitter struggles will occur in most countries unless there is a rapid increase in productivity to enable the workers' expectations to be met at least partly. It is this aspect of economic growth which makes the strongest appeal to employers and Ministers. Professor Lewis nevertheless contends that economic growth does not always reduce strife. It may, indeed, disrupt stable social relationships, arouse feelings of envy and jealousy, and precipitate conflict.[9]

Professor Mishan, in his scathing attack on economic growth, can see no advantages in it at all except for 'an indigent country', that is an overpopulated country in which the mass of the people struggle for a bare subsistence. Britain, he asserts, is not that sort of country.[10] Professor Mishan concentrates his attack on the costs of economic growth, and looking at these he can see no possible benefits to counterbalance the overwhelming damage which economic growth has inflicted on England's green and pleasant land. The politicians, moreover, in their compulsive struggle for power, ignore the new sources of social conflict and discontent which stem directly from the material prosperity of recent decades.[11]

Economists of the classical school assume without question that economic growth is not merely desirable, but essential to progress. Professor Hayek, a contemporary example, wrote that 'while in former times the social evils were gradually disappearing with the growth of wealth, the remedies we have introduced are beginning to threaten the continuance of that growth of wealth on which all future improvement depends'.[12] It is astonishing that a man who had lived for many years in Chicago could fail to see that the immense growth of wealth in the United States had failed to prevent or reduce racial conflict, violence, drug addiction, terrifying crime rates, slums, corruption and other evils which afflict American life. A New Zealand author has expressed the view that the continued survival of the welfare state is likely to depend on economic development, for its demands on current production are too heavy to be satisfied for long unless production expands steadily.[13]

Sir Arthur Lewis has given by far the most balanced and searching appraisal of the advantages and disadvantages of economic growth in the appendix to his great book on the subject. Among the benefits he mentions are that it enables people to choose between more goods and services or more leisure; that it relieves women of much drudgery and gives them the opportunity to become full human beings; that it enables people to afford the luxury of humanitarian activities. But he is fully aware that many people dislike the attitudes and institutions which are necessary for economic growth, and prefer stability to the restlessness and constant change which accompany growth. They dislike, among other things, what he calls 'the economising spirit', and feel that it makes excessive demands on people's nervous energy and their chances of happiness. There is much more in this summing up which leads Lewis to the conclusion that 'economic growth is desirable, but we can certainly have too much of it, more than is good for spiritual or social health, just as we may have too little of it'.[14] In his view excessive growth can result in, or be the result of, excessive materialism, excessive individualism, excessive mobility of population, excessive inequality of income, or the like. 'It may not be wise', he advises, 'for a nation to increase its rate of growth above the current level, for this may involve substantial costs in social or spiritual terms.'[15] Each situation must be appraised separately.

Sir Arthur Lewis was not addressing his remarks to the position of any particular country, but generalising in a manner intended to apply to all countries irrespective of the stage of their development or of any particular point in their history. He did not perceive any necessary connection between economic growth and happiness, though a connection could exist if wants remained fixed and resources increased. But this does not occur, and he declares that there is no evidence to show that the happiness of individuals increases as their incomes grow, or that the rich are happier than the poor. On the other hand, increasing wealth does not make people less happy.[16]

Even the most single-minded believer in the sanctity of economic growth would scarcely be prepared to equate the Gross National Product with human happiness. Obviously poverty of a kind which results in starvation, malnutrition, infant mortality, premature death, squalor, homelessness and other forms of misery, can cause great and prolonged unhappiness, which could be alleviated by an increase of wealth. But happiness is a positive state which is influenced by many imponderable factors, both hereditary and environmental, such as marriage and family life, relations between parents and children, work, love, friendship, personality and temperament, health, a sense of freedom and the opportunities for self-expression. Welfare is a far more manageable and serviceable concept, yet it too is not measurable as a whole, though many of its elements can be quantified.

While politicians, industrial leaders, economists and journalists talk and write as though economic growth were the supreme good at which the nation should aim, an international group of scientists, technologists, demographers and experts of other kinds belonging to the Club of Rome have sponsored a report which indicates that unrestrained growth is the supreme evil. The report declares that if the exponential growth of population, industrialisation, pollution and the consumption of natural resources continue at their present rates, a major collapse of civilisation will occur in the not distant future, resulting in a vast loss of life and a drastically reduced standard of living. The report covers the entire globe, and if the predicted collapse were to occur, no country could escape the dire consequence.[17]

The report attacks what the authors assert is the wholly false assumption that the environment will permit the unrestricted expansion of population, consumption, land development, the use of resources, and the inevitable pollution.[18] The only possible method they see of avoiding exponential growth and collapse is by keeping constant population and capital, the key factors in economic and social growth.[19]

The report is a piece of doomsmanship which should not be taken too seriously. Sir Eric Ashby, former chairman of the Royal Commission on Environmental Pollution, has remarked that if you feed doom-laden assumptions into computers, such as that pollution could increase to a level that would nearly halve the span of human life, it is not surprising that they will predict doom.[20] In any event the recommendations in the Club of Rome report that population and capital accumulation should not be allowed to increase could not be carried out.

A very different view is taken by Professor Beckerman, an economist who has served on the Royal Commission on Environmental Pollution. He agrees that many components of welfare are not reflected in the Gross National Product, and concedes that various forms of pollution, such as nitrogen oxides in the air, aircraft noise, an increase of pesticides and insecticides, and an extension of derelict land, have been getting worse owing to economic growth.[21] But he contends that this is due to the absence of appropriate policies about the way in which the fruits of economic growth are used and distributed. In short, he dissents from the idea that economic growth must *necessarily* lead to increased pollution. Where it does so, it is due to resource misallocation. Moreover, pollution is more likely to be reduced in a situation of economic growth than in one which is not growing. He also asks why we ignore improvements in the environment which are directly or indirectly the result of economic growth. Among those which have taken place during the past century are the sanitary conditions of towns, improvements in water supply and sewage disposal, better working conditions, and progress in housing and slum clearance.

Professor Mishan's attack on economic growth is directed at the situation that exists in Britain. He argues with great force that the leaders of business and government continue to give primacy to the indices of economic performance, and assume that these reflect the general good. If, however, we consider such matters as pollution, the growth of social conflict, the rise in divorce rates, the breakdown of authority among the young, the increase of violence and other symptoms of malaise, we should realise that our preoccupation with index economics has led us to a state of social deprivation.[22]

It appears that in Britain we have reached, or are approaching, a stage in which the causes and the consequences of economic growth, whether actual or anticipated, are meeting with increasing resistance from growing numbers of citizens.

Some of the developments aimed at economic growth which arouse the strongest opposition are those which disrupt or pollute the environment. A prime example are urban and rural motorways cutting ruthlessly through houses or shops, green fields or woodland, whether elevated or at ground level, producing noise, smell and visual disruption. The immense despoliation caused by a major airfield is perceived as the environmental effect of one factor expected to contribute to economic growth. Whole communities are vigorously opposing the disruption of areas (such as Covent Garden in the centre of London) for which drastic plans of economic growth and physical redevelopment have been prepared.

In his powerful onslaught on the costs of economic growth, Professor Mishan is in no doubt that the disamenities of economic development are so great and so unavoidable that we must choose between growth or welfare.[23] He does, however, make several constructive proposals for mitigating or preventing some forms of pollution by legislation or the imposition of financial obligations on those responsible.

Environmental disruption is not a new phenomenon. Air pollution was a cause of complaint as far back as the thirteenth century. The pollution of ponds and rivers was a frequent occurrence long before the industrial revolution. But in the present era the vast multiplication of causes and effects of environmental disruption have reached a stage in which they have reduced the well-being of millions of men and women and unless restrained could ultimately threaten the conditions on which human survival may depend.[24]

The impact of modern technology on the environment has been described at length by many observers. Max Nicholson points out that the frustration and dismay formerly felt only by naturalists and lovers of natural beauty when they witnessed the damage inflicted by technology as it spread from the towns to the countryside has come to be shared by millions of ordinary citizens who see and feel the degradation of the environment as it yields to the ruthless demands of the new technology.[25]

There is now a large and increasing literature on the deterioration of the environment, both urban and rural. In one of the better books on the subject John Barr analyses the impact on our eyes of rural squalor, urban squalor, and mobile squalor; on our ears by noise on the ground and in the air; on our nose by pollution; and on our taste and touch by other agents. Rural deterioration is caused by the intrusion of inappropriate and inharmonious elements which degrade the landscape, such as electricity transmission lines, badly-sited and poorly-landscaped transformer and power stations, derelict mineral workings with abandoned mines, quarries and spoil heaps, gas holders, factory or workshop buildings, farm buildings in a neglected condition or repaired with corrugated iron, Nissen huts used for mushroom growing, untidy and ugly residential premises. We may also include ill-conceived forestry with its endless rows of conifers; and badly designed, monotonous rows of council houses in the suburbs and villages. We must now also anticipate the immense developments of oil and natural gas, the exploitation of which will be regarded as infinitely more important than the protection against vandalism of the West Coast of Scotland, or of the national park which skirts the Pembrokeshire coast, or any other area of natural beauty.

The so-called 'recreation industry' is itself a major danger to any rational enjoyment by town dwellers of their enlarged opportunities for leisure and mobility, for it has infested many stretches of the coast with holiday bungalows, caravan sites, prefabricated cafés, garages and petrol stations, ice-cream kiosks, garish funland centres and other attractions which destroy the beauty of many lovely seaside resorts or inland towns in the west, south-west and other parts of Britain.[26] Several hundred miles of the coast are spoilt beyond redemption.

The degradation of towns and cities is due to causes different from those responsible for the deterioration of the rural or semi-rural environment. Foremost is the decline of civic design, which in the past created the most harmonious and satisfying townscapes. In London we had the great achievements of Regent Street, designed by Nash as a single entity, the terraces in Regent's Park, the splendid squares in Bloomsbury, Mayfair and Belgravia. Regent Street has been demolished and replaced by mediocre commercial buildings; the Bloomsbury squares have lost their unity of design and are being rebuilt in penny numbers. What was called architectural good manners formerly led architects to design buildings which harmonised with others nearby. Today, architects – possibly spurred on by their clients – seek to conflict with neighbouring structures, so that the end-result is little more than a jumble of edifices unrelated to one another.[27] Architecture itself is in a degraded state in Britain, with the upturned slab as the typical pattern for the office building, the block of flats or the hotel, using materials, elevations and designs which are the common currency of modern building in almost every country. There is scarcely a truly regional or even national style of architecture left in the world today.

Another great offender against the urban environment is the highway. Its main function is to act as a channel through which a ceaseless torrent of motor vehicles passes. A secondary function associated with the first one is to provide parking accommodation for the motor vehicles when they are at rest. Every street vista is blocked and destroyed by the intrusion of a stream of cars, taxi-cabs, lorries, vans and motorbuses. No less offensive to the eye is the street furniture and the communication symbols: the traffic lights, the zebra crossings, the winking pedestrian crossings, the yellow lines, the white lines, the signboards both large and small, the parking meters, the public off-street garages, the one-way-only notices, the no-entry signs, the railings to obstruct pedestrians: all this ugly impedimenta has contributed in varying degrees to the degradation of the townscape.

Lewis Mumford wrote some years ago that the current American way of life is based on the religion of the motorcar, and that the sacrifices people are prepared to make for this religion are quite irrational.[28] In the United States the religion has not quite such a firm hold since the difficulty of using automobiles in the giant cities has become apparent; but in Britain, as in most western countries, the faith is spreading rapidly among all classes. In Manhattan many residents have given up their cars owing to the difficulty of using them, and underground and surface railways are beginning to come back into popular favour, particularly with commuters.

The motorcar is a principal cause of the assault on our sense of smell, with its fumes and odours, whether produced by petrol or diesel fuel. This disamenity is less serious than the toxic effect of sulphuric acid or carbon monoxide, but the fumes caused by the internal combustion engine pollute the air so that the streets are enveloped in a grey mist and the sunshine is obscured. Most of the dirt on motorcars (other than mud) is due to what is euphemistically called traffic film, which is another name for the deposits of exhaust fumes.

The motor vehicle is the chief generator of noise in towns and cities, and the worst offenders in this respect are heavy lorries, container vehicles, motor-cycles, sports cars, motorbuses and motor coaches, but the private car also contributes considerably to the total volume of sound. On urban roads which carry dense traffic loads the noise caused by motor vehicles persists more or less continuously for many hours every day, and is therefore a more serious assault on hearing than the noise emanating from aircraft, which is more infrequent except for those unhappy mortals who live near the flight paths of a busy airfield. The noise levels of the large jumbo jet aircraft are much greater than those of the earlier generations of aircraft.

The goals of the industrial system and of what is usually meant by economic growth lead inexorably to an increase of motor vehicles, especially of private cars, more and bigger motorways, more civil aviation, more oil refineries, more power stations, more petrochemical plants, more giant international airfields, more steel works, more filling stations, more factories, more office blocks, more hypermarkets, more of everything concerned in the processes of production and distribution of goods and services. These goals are bound to lead to more pollution, a further disruption of the environment, and a more acute assault on our senses.

The balancing of economic advantages flowing from certain kinds of development against amenity or aesthetic considerations is not likely to be achieved without widespread awareness of, and opposition to, the assault on our senses which can and does disrupt the urban and rural environment. A determination to restrain or oppose such assaults may involve a choice between economic and non-economic goods, or between different types of economic goods. Without an awareness of this kind it is unlikely that any significant changes of direction will take place.

We must not regard the disruption of the environment simply as a byproduct of capitalism. Much disamenity in Britain is caused directly by public authorities. The National Coal Board has been dumping more than two million tons of colliery waste each year over the cliffs on to the Durham beaches;[29] and a large number of huge colliery tips are to be found in every coalfield. The Ministry of Defence has been in the forefront in destroying rural and coastal amenities which it seldom restores when giving up the land.[30] The Ministry occupies 145 miles of coastline and 45 miles of estuary shores. The Lake District has been constantly threatened by attempts by Manchester and other cities not only to draw water from its lakes but to refuse access to them even to pedestrians. The new Wellington Barracks in London is as offensive an intrusion on the skyline surrounding Hyde Park as the Hilton Hotel.

A more significant fact is that environmental disruption on a large scale occurs in the Soviet Union and is similar in character to that which takes place in capitalist or mixed economies. This was freely admitted by Professor V. S. Semenov of Moscow at an international symposium on the subject held in Tokyo in 1970. The Russians themselves have expressed surprise that in a socialist country where the public interest is supposed to be supreme according to the constitution, the laws protecting the environment are broken with impunity by industrial executives.[31] A leading academician asks what are the causes which, in the Soviet Union, interfere with a rapid advance in such an extremely important field as the rational exploitation of nature.[32] The regime has been slow in dealing with air pollution, the discharge of oil in the Caspian Sea and in rivers, the misuse of water resources, reduced sunshine, noise and other disamenities.[33] In Czechoslovakia environmental control is as backward as in the non-socialist regimes of western Europe, North America or Japan.[34] It is clearly wrong, therefore, to regard environmental disruption as a result of capitalist enterprise intent only on maximising profit. It is rather a consequence of wholehearted concentration on production which is found in the USSR and other communist countries no less than in western countries and in Japan. One can even say that in western countries threats to the environment are often restrained or defeated by the efforts of conservation societies or public opinion, which have no counterpart in the communist regimes of Eastern Europe.

Many economists are now convinced that the social costs incurred by the processes of manufacture, extraction, etc., should be borne by the producer and included in the costs of production, thereby raising the price of the product and reducing demand. The sum allocated to social costs would be either the money spent on reducing or eliminating the disamenity or compensating those who suffer from it. This would do something to lessen environmental disruption caused by industrial processes, but would affect only a small part of the problem. Professor Mishan proposes a more far-reaching measure by giving individuals a legal right to amenity.[35]

The central government, local authorities and *ad hoc* bodies are already engaged in a wide range of activities directed towards the control or prevention of environmental pollution. Legislation confers a mass of regulatory powers on public authorities enabling them to prevent or restrict air pollution by domestic fires, factories, offices, etc.; to prescribe the maximum permitted pollutants that motor vehicles are legally allowed to emit; to regulate the noise of motor vehicles and aircraft; to control the dumping of toxic wastes on land; to regulate the use of chemical fertilisers and pesticides on farms, gardens and smallholdings; to prevent the dumping of worn-out motorcars, kitchen equipment and farm machinery in unauthorised places; to forbid and penalise the discharge of oil in the sea; and to take steps to prevent other forms of pollution. There are numerous advisory committees endeavouring to keep the government aware of changes in the actual or perceived dangers; and several of the national research laboratories are working on selected aspects of the pollution problem.

The British effort compares favourably in several respects with that of many countries; but this is not saying very much. The Royal Commission on Environmental Pollution in their first report stated that, although a sense of responsibility for the natural environment is not new in Britain, there is still an immense amount to be done before we can even overcome the physical depredations left by the Industrial Revolution – and that occurred a long time ago.[36] 'Failing deliberate measures to control pollution and to repair past damage, there is likely to be a substantial deterioration of the environment in the years ahead and the quality of life in Britain will be correspondingly impoverished, despite an appearance of greater affluence.'[37] The Royal Commission's third report was devoted entirely to the severe pollution suffered by British estuaries and coastal waters.

The Royal Commission are concerned with a very wide range of pollutants, all of which can have serious adverse effects on the environment. The Commission were, however, careful to point out that the quality of the environment is also affected by matters falling outside their terms of reference, such as an increase of population, technological advances, economic growth and the spread of derelict land.[38] They might have added many other factors, including an increase in the number of motorcars, motor lorries, motorways and oil refineries.

The activities of the central government and other public authorities, and also of many responsible firms, in combating various forms of pollution are commendable and well-intentioned. The results are of varying effectiveness, and it is not possible to give an overall judgement. This is in any event unnecessary for the plain fact is that the disruption of the environment has been and is now proceeding at a pace that far exceeds the rate of preventive or remedial action at present taken by government or private agencies, except in a few instances such as the progress made under the Clean Air Act in the areas where it has been applied. The escalation of environmental disruption is indicated by the dramatic rise in the importance of the environment as a subject of high political importance at the local, national and international levels. It explains the appointment of a Secretary of State at the head of a great Department of the Environment by a Tory government and continued by its Labour successor; the calling of a United Nations Conference on the subject in Stockholm in 1972; and of the agreement between the US and the USSR to exchange information and share experience in this sphere. These are only a few straws in the wind.

The Stockholm Conference on the Human Environment was attended by 1,200 delegates from 110 countries. It approved 106 recommendations which were embodied in a so-called Action Plan. Several of them were too remote from the subject to be relevant to the discussion. For example, apartheid cannot usefully be considered in this connection any more than drug addiction, prostitution and other human evils. If everything is treated as contributing to the human environment, the discussion becomes so vague as to be meaningless.

It has now become clear that it is no longer possible to accept the goal of the industrial system – whether in a capitalist or communist or a mixed economy – in favour of unrestricted economic growth while regarding the environmental disruption which results from the attainment of that goal as merely an incidental disadvantage which can be removed by minor adjustments in the pricing methods whereby social costs are borne by the producer. We must recognise that many of the costs of environmental disruption and benefits resulting from its improvement lie outside or beyond the market mechanism and cannot be quantified or adequately measured in terms of prices. The fact that some kinds of pollution can be measured and costed does not affect the general proposition. The quality of the environment is an aggregate, and its degradation is caused by the combined effects of all the various factors which contribute to the total result, such as noise, polluted air and water, unpleasant smells, visual disamenities, overcrowding of streets, parks, shops, public transport, traffic congestion, and many others.[39]

A radical change of outlook will be required if we or any other nation are to achieve a welfare society. We must perceive the close relation between the processes of production and consumption and their effects on the environment. The naive mixture of admiration and envy for American productivity regardless of the acute problems which have arisen there of racial conflict, ghettos, crime, violence, drug addiction, squalor, poverty, and lack of public safety, shows how compartmental is our thinking and fragmented our outlook. Our political leaders, observes Mishan, have been impressed by the efficient organisation of industry, high productivity, the widespread use of automation, and the resulting affluence which provides families with motorcars, television sets, conditioned air, motorboats and yachts, on a scale unknown elsewhere. But they have ignored the sufferings of commuters by public transport, and the difficulties of those who commute by car, the mixture of pandemonium and desolation in the cities, the visual disorder of suburbs.[40]

More than twenty years ago a perceptive observer complained that we tend to be misled by American ideas of what constitutes prosperity. An English docker can now own a television set, a motorcar, and spend more on drink, food, tobacco and gambling, while his wife has a fur coat and his children can go to the cinema several times a week and consume innumerable ice-creams. 'But he still lives in the same squalid environment near the docks and the background and psychology of poverty are as before. Much of the increased prosperity of the working classes in recent years is of this kind – a semi-luxury gloss on a fundamental poverty below. The welfare state is just as prone as other industrial societies to misdirection of effort and to the kind of poverty that is due more to wrong ideas and to waste than to lack of material goods or to inequalities of wealth.'[41]

The loose talk about 'The Japanese Miracle' without reference to the environmental disruption which it has caused is based on a similar inability to discern a semi-luxury gloss on a fundamental underlying poverty. Anyone who knows Tokyo well is aware of the hardship caused to a large number of the citizens by bad housing, insufficient parks and playgrounds, grossly overcrowded commuter trains, lack of sewage plant and other disamenities.[42]

In 1968 an official survey conducted by the Tokyo Metropolitan Government showed 834,000 households living in sub-standard housing, representing 28·1 per cent of the registered households in the capital city, while 1,017,000 households, or 34·2 per cent, stated that they considered their housing accommodation to be inadequate. Allowing for an overlap between the two groups a total of 44·7 per cent of Tokyo's households were living in housing considered objectively or subjectively to be unsatisfactory. The main causes of dissatisfaction were – and still are – inadequate space, sharing of accommodation, living in non-residential premises such as garages, warehouses or shops, and poorly constructed buildings. Four years later, another official report stated that the housing situation had worsened. This report was a White Paper which declared that the housing problem is seriously affecting ten million citizens of Tokyo. It referred to shabby houses and poor environments irritating people's nerves, young and old alike; to whole families being crowded in a six-mat rented room measuring 9·9 square metres; to abortions carried out because the married couples concerned feared being evicted from rented accommodation if they had children; to dwellings constructed on crumbling or subsiding land; to walls so thin that every sound in adjoining rooms could be heard.[43]

A White Paper published in 1970 drew attention to the contemporary pollution problem, such as that caused by poisonous gas, smoke, smog, stench, waste fluid from factories, river pollutants, human waste and piles of refuse – all of which contribute to the aggravation of daily home life. A phenomenon selected for special mention was the catastrophic occurrence of photochemical smog which struck citizens of Tokyo with terror during the summer of 1970.[44]

The daily journey to work in Tokyo has become an ordeal which imposes ever increasing costs in terms of money, time, physical hardship and nervous energy. Until recently all buildings in the city were restricted to two or three storeys for fear of earthquakes, but Japanese engineers and architects are now constructing high-rise buildings which they believe will withstand even the most severe earthquake which may be expected according to previous experience. In consequence, skyscrapers of forty and more storeys are now appearing in the central city as office blocks and hotels. As the employment opportunities in the centre increase and the price of land rockets upwards to unprecedented heights, more and more workers are forced to seek homes at ever-lengthening distances from the centre. Residential settlements for commuters now extend to a radius of fifty kilometres. The unfortunate commuters are packed into the trains by the ex-wrestlers known as pushers, and the great majority of them are compelled by economic necessity to endure the ordeal because accommodation nearer their place of work is not available at prices they can afford.

'The Central Government considers Tokyo wealthy. It is not.'[45] This is the blunt official denial by the Tokyo Metropolitan Government of the assumptions about the so-called economic miracle so far as the finances of the capital city are concerned; and the statement is supported by statistics, charts and explanations.

It is not necessary to list in detail all the items which add to the discontents of Tokyo citizens, such as the rise in prices exceeding increases of income, or the fact that the sewerage system covers only 50 per cent of the most urbanised part of the metropolis (the special ward area), or the shortage of road space and parks compared to great cities in other countries.[46]

What is profoundly significant is the introduction in an official document of the expression 'the new poverty' to describe the position brought about by Japan's high economic growth. One aspect of this poverty is that people are constantly discontented while their desires are constantly inflamed. The enticing goods displayed in the shops, the incessant allure of leisure activities, the attraction of the motorcar, all encourage a high rate of expenditure on such seductive forms of consumption, yet leave the purchaser with a sense of starvation. In the sphere of housing, which bears many traces of the old poverty under bad conditions, people are excited by the mirage of house ownership by advertisements in newspapers, magazines and commercial radio. They then scrimp their expenditure on everything, even including food, in order to escape from the confines of a small rented wooden apartment to the freedom of 'my own house'. Another side of the new poverty is the worsening conditions of social life. 'While to the individual consumer life has seemingly been enriched, stimulated by human desires for consumption goods, what is called (in Japan) social investment, such as water supply, sewerage and parks, is not satisfied, a gross disproportion having developed between the two. Not only the natural environment, such as air, water and verdure, is being spoiled, but also living problems all over the city are aggravated because of insufficient waterworks, sewerage, refuse disposal, social welfare facilities, etc. Families which have long awaited adequate housing are affected by lagging city services such as water shortages, muddy roads even on fine days, and no refuse collection.' All this shows that the housing problem is not only a matter of finding dwelling places, but of the living environment as a whole. 'The problem of poverty in modern cities is that houses are built slowly and they have no relation to the other environmental facilities for living.'[47]

This passage reflects the disillusion with the economic miracle of the spectacular growth in the Gross National Product felt by many Japanese living in the great cities. It also shows that new criteria of wealth and poverty, and new standards of measurement, are likely to emerge in the near future. There are clear signs that conceptual changes of this kind have affected the thinking of outstanding political and industrial leaders. The main aim of Ryokichi Minobe, the elected governor of Tokyo since 1967, is to counteract the social and human costs of the capital city's huge economic and population growth. His comprehensive plan for a 'civil minimum' for the citizens of Tokyo is aimed at transforming the capital from a city dominated by industries to a city where men are supreme. He has explicitly declared that while highrise buildings and expressways are adding to the modern aspects of the metropolis, numerous disamenities incidental to an overgrown city are worsening the citizen's basic living environment.[48]

Mr Kakeui Tanaka, Prime Minister until 1974, has written a book advocating a drastic plan for restructuring and relocating the economy so that it would be directed not only to economic growth but towards making Japan a more agreeable country to live in. This would involve a shift from the heavy and chemical industries consuming large quantities of energy and raw materials to knowledge-intensive industries making greater use of man's wisdom and knowledge. These would include industries dependent on research and development, those producing computers, electric motorcars, anti-pollution equipment, business machines, and the fashion industries.[49]

It is surprising to find an equally decisive repudiation of conventional views held at the very centre of Japanese capitalism. A periodical published by Mitsubishi Heavy Industries (the title in English is MHI) contains a report of a round table discussion between two industrial leaders and a top civil servant in the Ministry of International Trade and Industry on 'The Reform of the Industrial Structure and the Responsibility of Enterprises'. In the course of the discussion Mr Toshio Shishido, Vice-President of the Nikko Research Center Ltd, proposed that an index such as NNW (net national welfare) should replace GNP; or that social indicators should be drawn up by the People's Livelihood Council. Mr Hisashi Kurokawa, President of the Mitsubishi Petrochemical Co. Ltd, conceded that business is no longer allowed to cause environmental disruption or other trouble to society, even if permitted by law to do so. Industrial undertakings must accept a change in their social responsibilities which now go beyond acting within the law. Mr Shishido said that businessmen should stop thinking that the primary object is to pursue profits. Hitherto, far too much technological development had been directed towards mass production, leaving technology aimed at preventing its bad effects lagging far behind. His concluding remarks, in response to a statement by the Editor that the goals of a welfare society should be explained and clarified, were that the concept of welfare was understood to mean the elimination of the wage gap and a more equitable distribution of income. About a decade ago, when the government announced its income-doubling plan, welfare was identified with increasing the social overhead capital. This drive to expand social investment continues but, he declared, 'it is now time to elucidate what welfare society we are striving for, taking into account the problems of health, the value of life and work'. The role and responsibility of enterprises in realising the welfare society is now much greater than in the past. Thus, 'it is wrong to think the government alone is responsible for creating a welfare society and that it means only higher pensions or more fiscal expenditures'.[50]

The experience of Japan suggests that the unrestrained pursuit of economic growth can result in such serious drawbacks that it may well be rejected in favour of goals more likely to create a welfare society. Japan may in time turn out to be a country from which the world has much to learn, not about the attainment of record rates of economic growth but about the consequences of so doing and the evolution of wiser policies. The revolt against pollution and urban degradation has been voiced by a former Prime Minister, the Governor of Tokyo, leading industrialists, economists, scientists and journalists.

A danger is that Japanese businessmen may try to export their pollution problems by building their pollutant-prone industrial plants in other countries in south and south-east Asia. This would be a shortsighted and immoral policy likely to cause resentment and probable nationalisation by the host countries.

Until recently the welfare state has been mainly concerned with individuals or groups suffering from poverty, unemployment, sickness and other vicissitudes. Attention and compassion have been focused on the handicapped, the disabled, widows, children, the sick and aged, the destitute and the underprivileged, whether as individuals or as groups. With the recognition of the overwhelming importance of the environment the welfare state is acquiring a new dimension, for pollution of the air, sea, rivers and land and other disamenities affect the whole community. From a concern with urban slums we have to come to recognise that many of our towns and cities, our semi-rural areas, and even villages, bear some of the stigmata which are found in slum districts, such as squalor, noise, smells, ugliness, unhealthiness, and a general degradation of the environment which affects all classes of society. It is now apparent that many of the disamenities we suffer from are collectively produced and can only be dealt with by collective action.

An easy answer to the many forms of environmental disruption which now confront us is to rely on an unlimited belief in the ability of science and technology to rescue us from the dangers and disadvantages which science and technology have brought, together with many great benefits. 'Man rushes first to be saved *by* technology, and then to be saved *from* it', is the way an American author puts the matter.[51] But a blind faith in the ability of technology to save us from the effects of a huge increase in the world's population, continuous growth, unlimited incremental pollution, an unrestricted armament race, and the reckless consumption of scarce resources is not warranted by any rational appraisal of the probability of technological trends and possibilities.[52]

It is quite possible to halt and reverse the tendency to environmental disruption if we have the will and the persistence to do so. What is needed is an understanding of the causal factors at work, and a willingness to adjust the order of priorities, to forgo certain benefits in order to obtain others. The single-minded pursuit of economic growth as an ultimate good in itself must be replaced by the notion of utilising growth to improve the environment, and of improving the environment even without economic growth.

In a modern city there are three major elements at work representing broadly the interests of economics, technology and welfare. The balance between these elements will largely determine the character of the city, or of separate parts of it or its environs. The centre of Rotterdam, for example, which was destroyed by bombing from the air in the Second World War, has been redeveloped in a delightful manner with low-built shops and dwellings, broad pedestrian walks containing flower beds from which wheeled traffic is excluded. Here the welfare element has been the main determinant.

A very different situation exists at Europort, the great new port situated to the west of Rotterdam on land owned by the city outside its boundaries. All the land bordering the Rhine delta has been sold for industrial purposes, mainly for oil refineries and petrochemical plants, including the world's largest refinery. A high degree of pollution has resulted and has spread to the twenty-three rural communes which surround the delta and on which housing estates have been built for the industrial workers. Most of the traffic using Europort is destined for Germany. Rotterdam has received substantial economic benefits combined with a heavy cost in disamenity and pollution of several kinds from this development. Situations of this kind may well arise in Britain in the late 1970s or early 1980s when the oil begins to flow from the North and the Celtic seas.

A city must have a sound economic base if it is to prosper and this means offices, markets, factories, shops, transport facilities, financial institutions, warehouses, etc. It must accept the unquestionable advantages of modern technology in regard to water supply, sewerage and sewage disposal, communications, the generation and distribution of power, lighting and heating, modes of transport and many other matters. But unless the welfare elements play an important part in the construction and development of the city, the quality of life of those who live in it will not be high.

The welfare element should therefore no longer be identified solely, or even mainly, with the provision of services for those in need, for in this context of the environment it has a much wider connotation embracing, indeed, the interests of all the citizens.

The physical structure should be regarded as having a pronounced effect on environmental welfare. If the structure contains a high proportion of buildings which delight the eye: of streets, squares or riverside walks which give pleasure because of the excellence of their civic design; of parks, public gardens and open spaces which are adequate in relation to the area and population of the city, well distributed and easy of access; of public buildings which inspire the citizen with a sense of pride; then it will be a positive addition to the welfare of inhabitants and visitors. Conversely, mean streets, slums, seedy rundown districts, ugly towe⸗

blocks of offices or flats, overcrowded sites, squalid shopping centres and such like, are elements of diswelfare.

Plans to transform the environment in town and country now frequently meet with strong opposition from those likely to be affected. The aspects of urban development which arouse most anger and opposition are those which are most alien to human values. Examples are the replacement of single-family houses, shops, etc., by highrise blocks of flats; the construction of towering office blocks in or near the inner city or residential suburbs in place of houses, shops, cinemas, theatres, pubs, clubs and other familiar landmarks; the driving of motorways through built-up urban areas or through quiet villages to the detriment of residents; the siting of airfields, oil refineries and similar installations in or near areas where life has been relatively tranquil. A common feature of these types of development is that they replace buildings which reflect human values by large-scale structures which by comparison appear inhuman and adverse to the well-being of the people whose lives will be closely affected.

During the 1960s and early 1970s property developers intent on maximising profits promoted larger and larger redevelopment schemes in or near the city centres, so that not only obsolete commercial, shopping and residential premises were replaced but many other buildings in good condition whose only offence was that without their inclusion the scheme would have been a smaller and less lucrative one.

A planning device resulting in the disruption of social life is the comprehensive redevelopment scheme. Among well-known examples in London are the bitterly opposed plans for Covent Garden, Soho, and Piccadilly Circus. The Covent Garden plan, as originally submitted to the Secretary of State for the Environment, would have destroyed two-thirds of an historic area of London in which a complex social, economic and viable pattern of life had evolved. The validity of the arguments put forward by the objectors to the scheme was largely recognised by the Secretary of State. The various schemes put forward to redevelop Soho would sweep away a unique mixture of foreign restaurants, craft workshops, shops selling musical instruments, flats, bed-sitters, offices and some dubious striptease shows and other forms of entertainment. Soho has for long been a picturesque, vital community with a goodly share of vices and virtues. To destroy it would be to deprive London of a well-known and much liked feature. Piccadilly Circus is generally regarded as the centre of the entertainment world in the West End of London. The first plan put forward by the

Westminster City Council, to whom the Greater London Council had unwisely handed over responsibility for its planning, met with almost unanimous opposition from every organ of public opinion, local and national, because the redevelopment permitted the replacement of existing buildings by enormous office blocks, an increase of traffic facilities for motorcars and the removal of the statue of Eros to an absurd position on a podium. It was predominantly a scheme to promote office building.

These examples suffice to show that opposition to development schemes are not merely based on the desire to protect buildings of architectural or historic interest, but to defend the way of life of an existing community. Usually it seems that the larger the scheme the more destructive its effects on the local community. This does not mean that what I have called human values must always prevail. It does mean that they must be taken into account. It may be that the scheme for the National Library to be built on seven and a half acres of land facing the British Museum is fully justified, despite the fact that it will displace a host of publishers, booksellers, art dealers and residents living or working in the area, on the ground that the public purpose of the object in view transcends in importance the unfortunate consequences which will result from the scheme. But this cannot be said for many of the schemes which have disfigured Bath, Lincoln, Newcastle-upon-Tyne and other fine cities.[53]

Attempts to resist environmental disruption are essentially conservative, and however successful they may be they will not improve the quality of life but only prevent its deterioration. If we wish to improve the quality of life we must deliberately aim at the recovery of human values in the physical structure of the environment.

Housing is a vital part of the physical structure; and it is easier to feel ashamed rather than proud of the housing position in many urban areas. Strange as it may seem, the worst slums are to be found in the metropolitan cities which are supposed to be the wealthiest urban centres. Homelessness has been on the increase in London for some years. Urban sprawl, bad housing and physical congestion, are typical features throughout the world.[54] Yet in most countries, including Britain, the giant cities are the most prosperous economic centres. They generally compare favourably with other parts of the country in regard to average income per capita, capital formation, economic growth, wage levels, employment and activity rates, the ownership of motorcars, telephones, refrigerators, washing machines, television sets, etc. In our materialistic age these are usually regarded as the indices of prosperity. They represent the basic terms of the economic calculus.

It would be foolish to dismiss these indices as unimportant in considering the level of welfare in a community. But it would be not only foolish but blind and stupid to regard these criteria as providing an accurate or comprehensive appraisal. We must look at other aspects of life such as the incidence of serious crimes, suicide, drug addiction, juvenile delinquency, divorce, baby battering, the neglect of, or cruelty towards, children, all of which are usually higher in proportion to population in the metropolitan cities than elsewhere. These are the outward expressions of unhappiness, frustration, alienation, and despair. There are no statistics of loneliness and solitude, but many observers believe they are more prevalent in the great cities than in smaller communities.

The journey to work is an experience which millions of men and women undertake on every working day. For most of them who live or work in the big cities, it is an ordeal which must be accepted as the unavoidable price to be paid for earning one's living in an industrial or commercial centre and residing a considerable distance away. The larger the city the greater the pressure on the transport system tends to be, and the more the commuter must pay in terms of time, money and physical or nervous energy. The overcrowding and discomfort of public transport at peak hours has induced commuters to take to the private motorcar, and this has led to packed highways, crawling traffic streams, endless bottlenecks and insoluble parking problems. When public authorities have responded to the motorist's demand for new or improved highways or motorways, the new facilities generate increased traffic, which quickly causes all the previous difficulties to return. Thus the lengthening journey to work imposes an increasing burden in real terms on the commuter, and indirectly on the community, whether it is made by private motorcar or by an overloaded and subsidised public transport system.

This has an important bearing on the quality of life, as anyone can see who observes the underground trains crowded with men and women with tired, strained faces, or watches the frenzied rush of human beings running to catch their trains in the main-line terminals at the end of the working day. The only remedy – apart from the construction of more new towns and town development schemes – lies in giving serious attention to the housing needs of low-paid workers nearer their work, either by the relocation of offices, shops, etc., or by allocating high-value land to low-priced housing. It is an uneconomic but essentially sound policy provided that care is taken to see that the housing is occupied only by transport workers, municipal employees and other workers who, by reason of the unsocial hours of their work or the low level of their earnings, are unable to live a considerable distance from their employment.

The great city has much to offer metropolitan man. It is here that we expect to find the fine public buildings designed by the greatest architects and adorned by leading artists. Every traveller remembers Notre Dame and the Louvre in Paris, the Town Hall in Stockholm, the Red Fort in Delhi, the Shogun's Palace in Kyoto, the Castles in Osaka. London has its full share of great buildings, but buildings alone do not make a city great. There must also be civic design of a high order, such as the Place de la Concorde in Paris, Trafalgar Square and the Embankment in London. And added to this there must be great public collections of pictures and sculpture, great libraries, museums, exhibitions, concerts, theatrical and operatic performances, and other cultural manifestations.

These are some, though by no means all, of the elements that contribute or detract from the quality of life, at least as it is lived in the great city. But, today, towns are becoming dominated by huge office buildings which grow ever taller; and blocks of flats, whether for the wealthy or for the lower income groups, soar higher and higher into the sky. Consider the effect of these two phenomena. So far as the faceless office block is concerned, at 5 o'clock the work stops, the lights go out, and the structure becomes dead until 9 o'clock next morning. The citizens cannot feel pride in their city if its pivotal points are taken over by enormous buildings which house the headquarters offices of banks, industrial or commercial firms, or oil companies. In an environment attuned to welfare, the faceless office blocks will not be permitted to dominate the city centre.[55]

So far as the high rise apartment block is concerned, it is now widely recognised that it is utterly unsuitable for bringing up young children, for the mother cannot see, much less supervise, her children when they are in the playground far below. Moreover, it induces a sense of isolation and loneliness, especially in the housewife, whether there are young children or not.

The broad conclusion is that we should plan and develop our cities in ways which will give the mass of citizens a good life in terms of health, enjoyment, convenience and beauty. Above all we must, whenever possible, retain the human scale as our yardstick. Moreover, we must try to enhance the sense of community among the inhabitants of our towns and cities. These objectives are difficult but not impossible to achieve. They are among the indispensable requirements of the welfare society.

The two most worthwhile developments in central London since 1945 are the Embankment buildings on the south side of the Thames and the Barbican. The Embankment development comprises the Festival Hall, the Hayward Gallery, the National Theatre complex and the riverside walk. All these fine buildings are on the human scale. The only adverse feature is the Shell skyscraper, partly because of its overwhelming size and partly because of its poor design. The Barbican development is attractive because it is comprehensive in a good sense by taking advantage of a severely bombed site to provide shops, restaurants, the City of London girls' school, the Guildhall School of Music, a new theatre for the Shakespeare Company, a museum, flats and houses, with walkways grade-separated from the adjoining highways. The scheme will indeed introduce a community life into the ancient city. The only adverse feature of the scheme is the excessive size of the enormous office blocks which overshadow the other buildings.

No one would believe that the planning and development of the built environment, no matter how excellent it may be, can solve many of the problems of the welfare state. On the other hand, unless the physical environment is a good one a welfare society cannot be attained. We must, however, be clear about the importance of the environment. Equality will not by itself ensure a good environment, nor will affluence, nor will socialism, nor will economic growth, nor will freedom, nor will *laissez-faire*. The physical and social environment is a separate dimension in its own right, though it has close connections with poverty, the social services, the cultural level of the community, demographic factors, the state of the economy and public policy. The creation of an improved environment should rank high as one of the surer paths leading to the welfare society.

Finally, we should not forget that however wisely and well we may use the additional resources made available by economic growth in improving the physical environment, there are many elements of welfare which do not require any economic growth. Among them are peace, the reduction or elimination of violence, improved racial relations, better understanding between husbands and wives and between parents and children, a more creative system of education, less disruptive industrial relations, less hooliganism, less drug-taking and drunkenness. All these would help to attain the welfare society.

NOTES

1 See pp. 20–1.
2 See, for example, David F. Lomax, 'What Attitudes to Growth', *National Westminster Bank Quarterly Review* (February 1974), p. 21.
3 J. K. Galbraith, *The Affluent Society* (1958), p. 347.
4 K. Gunnar Myrdal, *Against the Stream* (1974), pp. 184–5.
5 See, for example, Wilfred Beckerman, *In Defence of Economic Growth* (1975), p. 77.
6 Galbraith, op. cit, p. 351.
7 *Towards Equality,* Alva Myrdal Report to the Swedish Social Democratic Party (1971), p. 13; Galbraith, op. cit., p. 97.
8 Beckerman, op. cit., p. 32.
9 W. Arthur Lewis, *The Theory of Economic Growth* (1955), p. 423.
10 E. J. Mishan, *The Costs of Economic Growth* (1967), p. 4.
11 ibid., p. xviii.
12 F. A. Hayek, *The Constitution of Liberty* (1960), pp. 304–5.
13 J. V. T. Baker, 'Social Services and Economics Development' in *Welfare in New Zealand,* K. J. Scott (ed.) (1955), pp. 71–2.
14 Lewis, op. cit., p. 426.
15 ibid., p. 429.
16 ibid., pp. 420–1.
17 Dennis Meadows, *The Limits to Growth* (1972), *passim.*
18 ibid., pp. 185 et seq.
19 ibid., p. 175.
20 In a review of *Only One Earth: The Care and Maintenance of a Small Planet* by Barbara Ward and René Dubos, *Spectator* (27 May 1972).
21 Beckerman, op. cit., pp. 77–9, 105.
22 E. J. Mishan, 'Thinking of the Future' in *Fears and Hopes of European Urbanisation* (1972), pp. 102–3.
23 E. J. Mishan, 'Economic Priority: Growth or Welfare', *Political Quarterly,* Vol. 40 (1969), p. 79. Reprinted in William A. Robson and Bernard Crick, *The Future of the Social Services* (1970).
24 K. William Kapp, 'Environmental Disruption', in *A Challenge to Social Scientists,* Proceedings of International Symposium on Environmental Disruption, Shigeto Tsuru (ed.) Tokyo (1970), p. 4.
25 Max Nicholson, *The Environmental Revolution* (1970), p. 282.
26 John Barr, *The Assault on our Senses* (1970), pp. 10–11.
27 For a diagnosis of this decline see Lionel Brett, 'The Things We See' quoted by Barr, op. cit., p. 28.
28 Lewis Mumford, *The Highway and City* (1964), p. 214.
29 Steps are being taken to stop this pernicious practice.
30 See the Reports of the Defence Lands Committee 1971–3, Cmnd 5364 (1973), and Cmnd 5714 (1974).
31 Shigeto Tsuru (ed.), Proceedings of International Symposium on Environmental Disruption, Tokyo (1970), p. 164; Marshall I. Goldman quoting *Soviet Life* p. 171.
32 ibid., pp. 171–2.
33 ibid., pp. 164–9, 172–3.
34 ibid., pp. 74–84.
35 'Economic Priority: Growth or Welfare', *Political Quarterly,* Vol. 40 (1969), pp. 85–9.
36 Cmnd 4585 (1971), para. 30.

37 Cmnd 4585 (1971), para. 35.
38 ibid., para. 124 (5).
39 K. William Kapp, 'General Issues and Methodological Problems', in *A Challenge to Social Scientists*, Proceedings of International Symposium on Environmental Disruption, Shigeto Tsuru (ed.), Tokyo (1970), pp. 9, 13.
40 Mishan, *Costs of Economic Growth*, p. 7.
41 N. A. Smith, 'Theory and Practice of the Welfare State', *Political Quarterly*, Vol. 22 (1951), pp. 373–4.
42 *Sizing up Tokyo*, A report on Tokyo published by the Tokyo Metropolitan Government (1969), pp. 168–9.
43 ibid., p. 43; *Tokyo's Housing Problem*, published by Tokyo Metropolitan Government (1972), Chapter 1.
44 *Tokyo Fights Pollution: An Urgent Appeal for Reform*, published by Tokyo Metropolitan Government (1971), *passim*. See also *Sizing up Tokyo*, pp. 75–84.
45 *Sizing up Tokyo*, p. 24.
46 Tokyo has a per capita park area of 1·57m² compared to 22·8m² in London, 19·2m² in New York and 9·7m² in Moscow. The road ratio in Tokyo is also greatly below that in Washington DC, New York, Paris and London. *Sizing up Tokyo*, pp. 24 et seq.
47 *Tokyo's Housing Problem* (1972), pp. 5–6.
48 Foreword by Governor Minobe to *Tokyo for the People: Concepts for Urban Renewal*, published by Tokyo Metropolitan Government (1972).
49 Kakeyi Tanaka, *Building a New Japan* (1973), p. 66 and *passim*. Industry would be directed to five great coastal parks constructed at specified places in Hokkaido, Honshu, Shikoku and Kyushu. The islands would all be linked together by rail and road systems.
50 MHI, No. 8 (1973), pp. 7–8.
51 Gerald Sykes, 'A New Salvation, A New Supernatural', in *Technology and Human Values* (1966), published by the Center for the Study of Democratic Institutions.
52 Meadows, op. cit., p. 154.
53 An excellent article on these examples was by Christopher Booker entitled 'Enough to this Orgy of Ruin' published in *The Daily Telegraph* (27 August 1974).
54 William A. Robson and D. E. Regan (eds), *Great Cities of the World: Their Government, Politics and Planning* (3rd edn, 1972), pp. 122–3.
55 See William A. Robson, *The Heart of Greater London* (1965), a Greater London Paper published by the London School of Economics and Political Science.

Chapter VII

Economic Policy
in the Welfare State

Government intervention in the economy is ubiquitous and is of major significance, even in countries that cannot be classed as welfare states. It is, indeed, virtually impossible today to find a government which follows a *laissez-faire* policy. I shall endeavour in this chapter to show what economic policies are conducive or necessary to the promotion of welfare and to distinguish them from those which can only be justified on other grounds.

We have already noted in an earlier chapter that social insurance and social assistance are two of the most important social services. But they do no more than meet the needs – and often only the bare subsistence needs – of individuals when they are suffering from the common vicissitudes of life, such as unemployment, sickness, invalidity, widowhood or orphanage. The limited value of income-maintenance devices to deal with mass unemployment, on the scale which occurred during the great depression in the years between the two World Wars, led to a policy of full employment being adopted by the wartime coalition government.

The avoidance of massive unemployment is clearly a welfare objective when we consider the misery, hardship and waste of human resources caused by prolonged unemployment. When the policy of full employment was adopted, the question of how it relates to inflation was not perceived. High rates of inflation have become widespread in recent years and there is much controversy among economists about the causes. No government has so far managed to achieve full employment without producing a high rate of inflation, and no economist has proposed a remedy for inflation which will not *inter alia* cause a substantial increase of unemployment.

No one would suggest that a welfare state must choose between unemployment and inflation stated in these crude terms. The only sensible approach would be expressed in quantitative terms; for example, how much inflation is acceptable in order to avoid unemployment above a specified level, or how much unemployment would be tolerated in order to keep inflation below a certain figure? I do not intend to suggest the answers to this difficult question, but the following observations may be relevant. The two evils of unemployment and inflation do not necessarily afflict the same persons, or at least not to the same extent. Unemployment may hit a particular industry or group of industries more than others, or it may affect certain areas of the country. The older and more infirm workers, immigrants, and the less competent, are likely to suffer most. Inflation causes most hardship to pensioners and persons on fixed incomes, to women in one-parent families, to workers in the unorganised industries, and to those in occupations which cannot bring much pressure to bear on the economy. Contrast in this respect the position of dockers or railwaymen with those of kitchen porters or hairdressers, for example.

Another aspect of the full employment doctrine has begun to show itself in recent years. This is the policy which a government may follow for political reasons of keeping men at work regardless of the purpose. The Concorde supersonic aircraft is a classic example of this. At what point of wild extravagance will a British or French government be prepared to abandon the Concorde and cut the huge losses resulting from the project? At what point will the trade unions concerned be prepared to accept a termination without embarking on industrial action spreading through the aircraft or engineering industries? At what point will the aircraft manufacturers' lobby stop its loud cries about the need for Britain to undertake 'prestige' projects of this kind and the value to our economy of the unspecified fallout from advanced technology in this field? It is difficult to see the contribution which the Concorde project has made or will make to economic prosperity, and impossible to see in what way it has enhanced the nation's welfare.

Another recently emerging aspect of our preoccupation with full employment is the trade union strategy of opposing any attempt to close bankrupt or inefficient or non-viable undertakings by means of sit-ins, work-ins, lock-ins, seizure of assets, demonstrations, delegations to Ministers and other forms of pressure. These have affected the Triumph motor-cycle works, the Scottish plant of the *Daily Express* newspapers, the Upper Clyde shipyards, and was attempted at one of the largest Ford factories. It has extended to the proposed abandonment by Hawker Siddeley of a new aircraft which is scarcely off the drawing board. These activities are an extension of the notion of vested interests from the sphere of property to the sphere of jobs. If successful, they will result in economic rigidity, which is an industrial cost, not a benefit. Where government aid is invoked, the underlying assumption is that subsidisation at the expense of the taxpayer is a practical alternative to economic viability which is fully justified if it keeps men at work.

A rational approach to this question is to distinguish between production which is intended to be viable, such as the manufacture of goods which are sold in the market, and the production of goods and services which are not intended to be sold in the market. In this latter category is a vast range of public works, from building hospitals to constructing sewage works or freeing our rivers from pollution. In this latter category one can see clearly the welfare aim, and it is here that the full employment policy coincides closely with the goals of a welfare society.

The doctrine of full employment remains of central importance, but today it needs considering in the wider context mentioned above. It is no longer sensible to give full employment the absolute priority it has hitherto enjoyed, without regard to (1) the level of inflation, in so far as this is due to the government expanding the money supply in order to maintain or increase the volume of employment; (2) the burden imposed on taxpayers in order to maintain employment in industries which are not viable without subsidies; (3) the rigidity imposed on the economy if specific types of employment with particular firms are regarded as inviolable, no matter what their financial results. These are matters which closely affect the relation of full employment to welfare.

Economic planning has not so far contributed much to the progress of the welfare state in Britain, although in theory it should form an authentic instrument of welfare policy. Major matters such as the creation and location of new towns, the help given to development areas and special development areas by the central government, the controls exercised by the government over the location of industry and office development, the siting and construction of motorways: these and similar matters have been planned by the relevant Ministries usually as separate questions rather than as parts of a comprehensive plan. Some matters which should have been planned nationally, such as the network of airfields for civil air transport, have never been planned at all. The only comprehensive national plan was drawn up by Mr (as he then was) George Brown in 1965 when he was Secretary of State for Economic Affairs, but it was stillborn. That was the first and last attempt at a comprehensive economic plan. Some of the regional plans, such as the one for the south-east, deal with economic questions as well as social, political or land-use questions, and eventually the whole of the United Kingdom is expected to be covered by such plans.

It is doubtful if the economy would have yielded a more satisfactory performance if further attempts at comprehensive national economic plans had been made after the failure of the George Brown plan. There are, however, a number of matters which require the determination of policy and planning at the national level. They include (in addition to those mentioned above) national parks and the preservation of amenities of national importance; the development of major ports; inland waterways; water supplies and large-scale drainage and irrigation schemes; the development of power resources of all kinds; the protection or expansion of agriculture and husbandry; the promotion of industrial or trading estates; the development of the nationalised industries and services; housing policy; higher education; publicly-conducted or state-supported research and development; major highways and bridges. Many of these matters are already subject to sectoral plans, such as those drawn up by British Rail and the British Steel Corporation for the development of their respective industries, and these have been approved by the Ministries concerned. It is, however, the balancing and co-ordinating aspects of overall planning which are likely to promote welfare, and it is this which has so far been lacking in Britain.

What is the role of public enterprise in the welfare state? This question requires careful consideration, because there are many different motives for nationalisation, and while some of them are related to welfare others are not. Some socialists adopt a straightforward Marxist view that the class struggle can only be decided in favour of the workers if economic power is transferred to the state, and they see nationalisation as the best method of doing this. The late John Strachey, MP, expressed the traditional Marxist position that 'no decisive advance to socialism can be made without breaking the class monopoly in the ownership of the means of production by changing society's relations of production'.[1] A similar view underlies the demands of the left-wing of the Labour Party at the present time for more nationalisation. Certainly Mr Tony Benn's principal motive would seem to be his desire to transfer more economic power from private enterprise to the Government or to the trade unions. This may be a valid socialist aim, although that is disputed by several eminent socialists, but it does not qualify as an objective of the welfare state. If it did, the communist countries of Eastern Europe would rank as the fore-most welfare states, whereas they are neither welfare states nor welfare societies for reasons I have already explained.[2]

Many trade union members and officials support proposals for the nationalisation of their industry because they believe that under public ownership they would be able to exert greater pres-sure on the Government to subsidise failing industries or keep in being plants threatened with closure, than they could bring to bear on commercial companies. This is not necessarily a true supposition,[3] but in any event it is not a welfare aim.

The Attlee Government's nationalisation policy in 1945–51 sprang from a conviction that socialism required the public owner-ship and operation, in the interests of the whole community, of the basic industries providing fuel, power, transport, and the essential raw materials on which the entire economy depends. But in addition to this general belief, the industries concerned with coal, transport, gas, electricity and civil aviation were separately examined in order to indicate to the public the reasons why each of them had been chosen for transfer to the public sector.[4] These included such matters as the need for improved organisation in the gas and electricity industries, or the need to secure co-ordination of trans-port services. Backward industries such as coal and the railways were taken over with the intention of modernising and rationalising them and investing much larger sums of public money in their improvement than the companies which owned them were willing to raise. The coal industry and the railways have made great advances in efficiency and productivity since nationalisation, and the position of the miners and the railwaymen has been greatly improved, although British Rail is, and will probably remain a loss-making industry.

The nationalisation programme of the Attlee administration was fully justified on the ground that with the possible exception of steel the industries involved formed part of the main infra-structure, and it is the duty of a welfare state to see that the infrastructure is adequate to contemporary needs, which it certainly was not in 1945.

The essential components of the infrastructure are: (1) public transport, comprising railways, airlines, motorbuses, underground or subway systems, ferries, etc., together with main roads, bridges, airfields, ports, harbours, railway terminals and similar facilities; (2) fuel and power supplies, whether coal, gas, electricity, oil or nuclear energy; (3) communications, comprising postal services, telephones and telegraphs; (4) water supply, sewerage, land drainage and irrigation. These industries require very heavy capital investment, not only initially but also for their continuous development. Nearly all of them are monopolistic by their very nature, and they also provide an essential service or product. They are mostly classed as public utilities. For these reasons they cannot be left to unrestricted private enterprise without exposing consumers to the dangers of monopolistic exploitation. In consequence, if public utilities are owned and operated by commercial companies, they are strictly regulated by legislation and administrative action designed to control prices and profits, to avoid discrimination, and to impose obligations to supply the public.

The general experience of public utilities operated by commercial companies is unsatisfactory, although there are a few extremely successful examples, such as the Bell Telephone System in the United States. Public regulation tends to be of a negative kind and is unable to compel a company to invest on a sufficient scale. Where a franchise is granted for a specified period, a company is not likely to be willing to invest funds unless it is assured of an extension of the franchise, and if the undertaking is in a poor condition this may be politically difficult or impossible. Some activities of public utilities aimed at economic or social development may be loss-making for some years, such as rural electrification of scattered farms, or air services connecting sparsely populated islands. Such services can and perhaps should be subsidised by the Government; but the latter may object to paying for specific services and prefer to transfer the entire undertaking to the public sector, thereby making it possible to average loss-making and profitable activities – despite the disapproval of certain economists of this practice. For these reasons the public utility type of industry or service should be publicly owned and administered in the welfare state.

A quite different kind of undertaking which should be in the sphere of public enterprise is the construction or development of new towns. The new town movement began in Britain as a means of achieving a better pattern of urban living than the vast overgrown industrial cities with their never-ending suburbs and the ever-longer journey to work. The aim of a new town, as conceived by Ebenezer Howard its originator, is to bring about a close and convenient relation between the workplace and the home, good housing at moderate prices, shopping facilities within easy reach of the housewife, a satisfactory complement of schools, clinics, libraries and other municipal institutions, and a wide range of recreational facilities. The classic model is a planned town of modest size surrounded by a green belt of countryside or woodland, or a brown belt of agriculture or horticulture. The most successful examples of new towns are those within easy reach of a large city, not in order to facilitate commuting but rather in order to make it unnecessary, for the basic principle is to bring together the home, the workplace, and the recreational facilities. These were closely integrated in former times, but with the growth of vast cities and the development of rapid transport, they became scattered and dispersed.

Most of the new towns constructed in Britain during the first phase of the post-war period were intended to relieve the congestion and to restrict the growth of the great city. Sir Patrick Abercrombie proposed eight satellite new towns for London in his plan for Greater London. In due course these were constructed (though not on the sites he suggested). In the 1960s a second wave of new towns was begun, the purpose, size and location of which are related to regional planning.

The new towns – or at least those not too far from a metropolitan city – have proved to be potent instruments of welfare. They have attracted business firms to locate or relocate within their areas factories, offices, shops, laboratories, etc., thereby affording employment for the local residents. They provide better living conditions for the inhabitants than they could obtain in the great city. They are freed from the necessity of making the costly, time-consuming, and exhausting daily journey to work. The new towns have contributed substantial benefits to their inhabitants and also to the great cities whose congestion they have eased. In addition, the new towns are now recognised as economic growth points. When complete, they provide a modest financial return on the capital investment provided from public money for their construction.

The great majority of new towns in the numerous countries which have constructed them have been planned, financed and developed by the state. There are, however, a few examples of private enterprise in this field. Kittimat is a town in Canada provided by a great commercial corporation for the workers in its aluminium plant. Kittimat is a poor example of a new town because the profit-seeking motive was dominant. Radburn in New Jersey is another private enterprise venture. The promoters were compelled at an early stage to sell off much of the land intended to be used for the new town, and today Radburn is mainly a housing estate for commuters completely embedded in the surrounding urban development. We may conclude that public enterprise in the promotion of new towns is a legitimate and desirable economic and social policy for a welfare state.

The relation of public enterprise in general to the welfare state and the welfare society is far from clear, apart from the sectors and projects discussed above. Sweden is an advanced welfare state, and the Swedish nation is a welfare society to a far greater degree than the British people. Yet the number of publicly owned industries in Sweden is small and insignificant, despite the fact that a Social Democratic Government has been in power for more than forty years. In Italy, on the other hand, there is a very large and thriving public sector, including *inter alia* nearly half of the engineering and metal-using industries, yet it is difficult to regard Italy as a welfare state or as a welfare society.

During the twenty-five years which have elapsed since the Attlee governments carried out the massive transfer to public ownership and administration of the infrastructure industries, there has been an almost continuous discussion within the Labour movement about what its policy should be on nationalisation and public ownership.[5] The opponents of what may be described as further nationalisation for its own sake have included the late Hugh Gaitskell, a former leader of the Parliamentary Labour Party, Mr Crosland, the group known as Socialist Union, the Co-operative Party and the TUC. Most of the participants in the discussion were concerned with such matters as the unwieldy size of the public corporations; other and more effective methods by which the aims of socialism could be achieved; the differing needs of manufacturing industries from those which had already been nationalised; recognition that the power of monopolistic ownership even when entrusted to public authorities can be open to abuse and indifferent to consumer interests; the notion that the control of power in the market through countervailing forces should be a major objective; and that diverse forms of social ownership should replace the nationalisation concept which critics have described as state capitalism.

For electoral purposes the Labour Party has proposed in recent decades the nationalisation of various industries such as cement, sugar, aircraft construction, machine tools, chemicals and insurance. But the main interest has been focused on state participation in the ownership of commercial companies and the method by which they can be controlled. Hugh Gaitskell advocated an extension of public ownership by means of the purchase of equity shares or their acquisition in settlement of death duties, or through the device of a capital levy. This would not require the state to exercise detailed control over an individual firm: in other words, he distinguished ownership from control.[6] Mr Crosland contended that a substantial change of ownership is not necessary to raise the standard of living, to promote social and economic equality, and to achieve other desirable goals. Indeed, a change of ownership will not ensure the realisation of these aims, but they can be achieved by appropriate controls.[7] In 1957 the Labour Party turned its back on further nationalisation and came out strongly in favour of Mr Gaitskell's policy of the state acquiring stocks and shares in large commercial companies. The object was to enable the community to participate in the substantial capital gains which accrue in normal times to the owners of the equity. The policy did not signify that the state would seek to control the companies concerned, but only that it would secure some of the substantial capital gains which would otherwise enrich the functionless private shareholder. This indicated the party's disillusion not only with public enterprise but also with public control of private enterprise.[8]

Strong support for this policy has recently come from Professor Sir Arthur Lewis, who is both an eminent economist and a committed socialist. In a public lecture delivered at the London School of Economics and Political Science in 1971 he declared that 'nationalisation by itself does nothing to ensure that private wealth will not grow even as nationalised industry itself grows.'[9] Purchase by the state of industrial assets from private owners leaves the latter as rich as before except that they now hold government securities. In his view, what matters more than anything else is the volume of public saving. If public saving is low, investment must be financed by private saving, and this means that private wealth will continue to grow. Therefore, the rate of growth of private wealth is determined primarily by whether saving is private or public, not by whether industries or firms are privately or publicly owned.[10]

Nationalisation, Lewis asserts, is compatible with economic growth, and able to lower the growth of private wealth, only if it is accompanied by a high rate of public saving. The main sources of public saving are the profits of public enterprise and the budget surplus.[11] Unfortunately, nationalised industries have generally failed to make a surplus on anything like the scale required to finance a high proportion of their investment needs. I have urged repeatedly that a major part of capital development in the nationalised industries should be financed out of surpluses made in the course of their normal trading operations, but this has seldom, if ever, occurred. In the private sectors joint stock companies are able under normal conditions to finance between two-thirds and three-quarters of their capital investments from retained profits and depreciation funds, but the public sector has never remotely approached this figure.[12]

The reasons for this failure are clear beyond a shadow of doubt. Governments have always exercised a strict control over the prices charged by nationalised industries, although in Britain they have no legal power to do so. Every government, whatever its political complexion, has intervened to restrain public undertakings from raising their prices or charges as long as possible regardless of increased costs. The Heath Government used the public corporations as instruments for keeping down the level of prices, with the result that all the nationalised industries in the domestic field were compelled to accumulate enormous deficits, amounting in the aggregate to about £1,000m. in 1974. Such discrimination against the public sector is misguided because it makes very steep price increases inevitable at a later stage. Above all, it is demoralising for the public corporations to be unable to meet their financial targets and to operate at heavy losses. It is also opposed to the Conservative Party's claim when in opposition that the publicly owned industries should be run on commercial lines.

Both of the major political parties have failed to use the budget as an instrument for public saving by keeping taxes up and current expenditure down. Conservative policy is to reduce taxation, while Labour policy is to increase expenditure on education, health, welfare and other social services. Hence, Lewis points out, the Labour Party would have to change its whole fiscal philosophy in order to become truly egalitarian. It would have to impose severe restraints on current expenditure and to urge nationalised industries to make much larger surpluses, which they could do only if they had greater freedom to raise their prices when this is rendered necessary by increased costs or the general level of prices.[13]

The failure of the public sector industries to yield substantial surpluses is only one of the grounds on which Sir Arthur Lewis opposes public enterprise. He refers to the disillusionment caused by the fact that nationalisation has not ended industrial strife. He writes also of 'its contempt for the consumer and its administrative rigidities'.[14] He believes that public ownership and public financing of production (through public saving) do not necessitate operation by a public corporation or other public authority, but are quite consistent with management by private enterprise, by the employees, by the consumers, or by the state, without violating the objective of restraining the growth of private wealth. I think Lewis goes much too far in his exclusive concern with public saving as the sole method of restraining the relative growth of private wealth and in regarding equalisation as the sole objective of public ownership. He fails to give any consideration to the extreme inefficiency of private management in the coal industry and the railways prior to nationalisation – an inefficiency which had much deeper causes than a lack of sufficient capital investment. To dismiss the achievements which have taken place in, for example, the gas, electricity and broadcasting industries with a few loose generalisations, is not a convincing appraisal of their performance. We should certainly experiment with alternative forms of management in the public sector, without assuming that the public corporations are unsatisfactory or that the alternatives are likely to be superior.

Nonetheless, Sir Arthur Lewis has drawn attention to an important and neglected aspect of economic policy which is relevant to the welfare state as well as to socialism. We have for years in Britain been precluded from embarking on many desirable public developments owing to lack of capital caused by insufficient saving. This applies both to the private sector as well as to the public sector. This may well be due to the superior attraction of spending as compared with saving in an era of high inflation. But whatever the cause, a higher rate of public saving would be extremely valuable as a welfare state policy.

Incidentally, Sir Arthur Lewis points out that the communist countries of Eastern Europe have had a rapid rate of economic growth not because they have socialist regimes or planned economies, but because they have achieved high rates of saving and investment, accompanied by severe restrictions on personal consumption, and a great development of education and training.[15]

I have referred earlier to Hugh Gaitskell's proposal that the state should acquire equity shares in profit-making commercial companies by various means, and the acceptance of this policy by the Labour Party in 1957.[16] Acquisition could take place by purchase, by acceptance in payment of death duties, or through a national superannuation fund. Sir Arthur Lewis sees it as a way of raising public saving, and urges that payment of corporation tax could be made in part by shares.

Underlying this policy is the concept of the state as *rentier*, which is not compatible with the philosophy of the welfare state. The result would lead to the functionless private shareholder being replaced by the functionless public shareholder. Moreover, if the state were to have a substantial interest in the profitability of certain companies, the government could be placed in an invidious position in such matters as fiscal policy, or the purchase of supplies. Furthermore, in order to realise and maximise capital gains, the government would have to engage in frequent buying and selling of its holdings on the Stock Exchange in much the same way as any private shareholder or institutional investor. Would such a spectacle commend itself to members of the Labour Party who denounce all such financial operations as immoral speculation?

The notion of the state acquiring wealth for the sake of acquiring wealth, or, what amounts to the same thing, to prevent it from falling into private hands, has been severely criticised both by the Right and by the Left. The idea nevertheless continues to be advocated. The most damaging criticism has come from Socialist Union, which rejected the belief that the ownership of property is dangerous only in private hands. Experience has shown that even when entrusted to public authorities the power of ownership can be dangerous.[17]

There is much to be said in favour of mixed enterprise, and we may expect to see much more of it in Britain. One advantage in a welfare society is that mixed enterprise by its very nature reduces the conflict between those who support capitalism and the proponents of public enterprise. A mixed enterprise may be defined as an undertaking in which public authorities and private interests participate substantially both as owners of the capital and as directors or managers. Hitherto most mixed enterprises in France, Italy and Britain have consisted of subsidiary companies in which nationalised industries have an interest, although the most important single example here is British Petroleum in which the state has a majority holding.[18] The controlling or directing power of the public authority in a mixed enterprise can be exercised in various ways. The government or the public corporation may have a right to appoint directors to the governing board. They may have a right to veto or approve certain acts of the board, such as disposal of the company or its assets or a merger, etc.; or they can lay down the policy of the undertaking. This type of participation in major policy distinguishes a mixed undertaking from one in which the state has acquired only a minority financial interest in the equity.

The Labour Party's present policy is to introduce a new relationship between the government and industry rather than to embark on a deliberate policy of creating many more mixed undertakings on the lines mentioned above. The new relationship will consist primarily of planning agreements entered into voluntarily between the Department of Industry, leading companies and the trade unions concerned. These agreements will aim at ensuring that the companies conform with the government's economic priorities in return for an assurance that the government will approve industrial developments for which permission is sought in regard to location of new factories etc., and will provide also financial assistance if this is requested. The agreements will include such matters as price control, the level of domestic and export sales, the scale of investment in the UK, regional employment policy, industrial relations and product development.

There is nothing inherently objectionable or in conflict with the goals of a welfare state in these proposals. If a more coherent interaction can be achieved between government policy and the plans, programmes and practices of leading industrial firms, this would be an advantage. Similarly, if the conflict between the unions and some major industries can be abated and a more harmonious relationship introduced, this will clearly be to the national advantage. What remains unclear is whether large joint stock companies and the Whitehall departments are capable of exercising the foresight required to predict with any precision or certainty such matters as the level of sales at home and abroad or the scale of proposed investment five years ahead, or what level of prices will be needed to keep the enterprise viable in an age of inflation. If all these vital matters can be foreseen and quantified by means of the agreements this will be a feat of no mean order. It will, indeed, be a surprising achievement. Whether they do or do not attain this aim, I see nothing in the new policy which is incompatible with the objectives of the welfare state. On the contrary, the more harmonious the relations between government, industry and the unions, the nearer we may come to being a welfare society. I know that some sceptics will say that such a get-together of the three participants may result in the exploitation of the consumer; but they surely forget that it is consumers who have been the chief sufferers in the almost incessant strikes, go-slows, work-to-rules, and overtime bans which have occurred in recent years.

Contemporary Labour Party policy on public ownership is more open to question. It is reasonable that when direct government aid is given to a company, the government should have the right to acquire in exchange a share in the ownership. Certainly if a British firm is in danger of being transferred to foreign ownership, the government should have the right to ask Parliament for power to take over the company. Natural resources, such as mineral rights, land required for development, oil and gas in the North and Celtic seas, are likely to be better protected and exploited for the benefit of the nation if they are in public rather than private ownership.

Beyond this, some of the Labour Party's proposals rest on shaky foundations. The ports are part of the infrastructure and should certainly be nationalised. But why should the ailing shipbuilding, ship-repairing and marine engineering group be taken into public ownership? The industry has been in almost continuous decline since the end of the boom years following the Second World War. A declining industry presents the most unfavourable conditions for nationalisation. The public ownership of the Italian shipyards has been one of the failures of public enterprise in Italy. This is a return to the old discredited policy of taking over the whole or part of any industry which is found to be 'failing the nation'. Several years ago I pointed out the futility of this policy, which would be likely to saddle the state with all the most inefficient, backward, contracting or stagnant industries.[19] The policy disappeared for several years from the Labour Party's programme but has recently reappeared.

The aircraft industry (including both air frames and aero engines) is also to be nationalised on the ground that like ship-building it cannot survive without massive government support. This is a vague term which could include the cost of developing and purchasing military aircraft, the development of new engines, or contributions to the launching costs of new types of civil aircraft. What needs to be shown is the evidence that the present system of subsidies is wasteful or unnecessary, and that the existing ownership of the industry results in less excellent design and technology and less efficient production than might be achieved under state ownership and control.

The extension of the public sector is, in future Labour Party plans, not to be confined to loss-making and subsidised industries such as the railways and shipbuilding, but will also include profitable sections of individual firms in industries where a public holding is deemed to be essential to enable the government to control prices, stimulate investment, encourage exports, create employment, protect workers and consumers from the activities of irresponsible multinational companies, and to plan the national economy in the national interest. Among the industries falling into this baleful category are sections of pharmaceuticals, road haulage, construction and machine tools, and the exploitation of oil and gas. Banking, insurance and the building societies are under consideration. Any assets hived off by the Heath Government, such as Thomas Cook, would be restored to the public sector. There is also the recommendation that twenty-five of the leading companies should be nationalised. Mr Wilson has publicly stated that he is opposed to this proposal,[20] but it remains in the policy statement.

One objection to this policy lies in the fact that investment plans must be initiated by the operating body, whether it is publicly or privately owned, for the simple reason that nowhere else is the necessary knowledge to be found. Investment by a commercial company cannot be stimulated if its prices are held down by government decree, *a fortiori* in a period of acute inflation. A second objection is that the problem in much of British industry is not how to create employment but how to increase productivity by eliminating redundant employees or rules restricting output. The prospect of these industries remaining profitable if subjected to the governmental controls referred to is likely to be small; and one essential lesson which emerges from this type of wishful thinking is that there is a limit to the number of public enterprises which can be subsidised by the taxpayer.

The general conclusion to be drawn from this analysis is that however desirable it may be for the government to keep down prices, increase investment, stimulate exports, create employment and protect consumers, it is seldom possible to attain these general objectives beyond what commercial considerations can achieve, without destroying the profitability of the undertaking, except where monopolies are preventing the exercise of competition.

Public enterprise can sometimes be justified in a welfare state in circumstances other than those discussed above. For example, if a firm which dominates an industry is using its monopolistic position to the disadvantage of consumers and the economy generally, that would be a good reason for taking it over. Again, where there is an existing or potential demand for a product which private enterprise does not attempt to satisfy, public enterprise should step in to fill the gap. A third example is that if prices are being held at an unduly high level through the activities of a price ring or some other type of cartel action, welfare policy would indicate that public enterprise should demonstrate the possibility of reducing prices or improving the service to the public. A fourth example is where the country is entirely dependent on imported supplies of a particular commodity, and private companies are unwilling to challenge this dependence, a public enterprise could be justified in attempting to substitute a home-produced product on a viable basis. The policies hitherto followed by the National Industrial Development Corporation in supporting such novel inventions as the hovercraft are excellent in principle and can result in either a public corporation or a commercial company being invited to co-operate with the corporation in exploiting and developing an invention. These examples are not exhaustive but they show some of the circumstances in which public enterprise can supplement and stimulate private enterprise and benefit the management, workpeople and consumers in a welfare state.

The Labour Party's programme on public ownership seems to be based on the desire to transfer power from the private sector to the government rather than on the aim of increasing welfare or prosperity. There is no indication of any measures to increase public saving or to reduce expenditure. Indeed, the social services have been expanded in various directions.

A more useful line of approach may be the announcement that existing nationalised industries are to be socialised. Unfortunately this is defined far too narrowly as making the management more responsible to the workers in the industry and more responsive to consumer needs. There is no mention about making the workers more aware of, and solicitous about, the needs of the economy, other industries and the general public, which have been totally ignored in recent years by trade unions and their members in the nationalised industries when engaged in collective bargaining and industrial disputes. In the private sector, also, there is a need for a greater degree of consumer protection and information than at present exists. The range of choice for consumers is being continually reduced as mass production methods are extended to more and more classes of goods.

The economic policy of a welfare society should aim at better industrial relations than those we suffer from in Britain. This embraces not only giving the workpeople through their representatives on the board of directors a voice in the decisions of management – a long overdue reform in Britain – but also trying to improve the productivity of industry. There is a need not only for more industrial democracy within the firm, but also for more industrial democracy within the unions.

NOTES

1 John Strachey, 'The Object of Further Nationalisation', *Political Quarterly*, Vol. 24 (March 1953), p. 74.
2 See p. 16.
3 The Nationalised Coal Industry suffered a massive contraction under plans initiated by the Labour Government in 1966.
4 See William A. Robson, *Nationalized Industry and Public Ownership* (1962), pp. 29–45.
5 I have described the views expressed by the principal participants in this discussion in some detail in my book *Nationalisation and Public Ownership*, ch. 16.

6 *Socialisation and Nationalisation* (1956), Fabian Tract No. 300, pp. 6, 34.
7 *The Future of Socialism* (1956), pp. 470–5; The Transition from Capitalism in *New Fabian Essays*, R. H. S. Crossman (ed.) (1970), p. 62.
8 *Industry and Society* (Labour Party pamphlet).
9 W. Arthur Lewis, *Socialism and Economic Growth* (1971), p. 10.
10 ibid., p. 11.
11 ibid., pp. 12–13.
12 Robson, op. cit., p. 307. The figures given above assume that there are no restrictions on prices or profits.
13 Lewis, op. cit., pp. 10, 13.
14 ibid., p. 14.
15 ibid., p. 15.
16 See *Industry and Society* and *Socialisation and Nationalisation*.
17 Robson, op. cit., pp. 466, 480–5.
18 See my article 'Mixed Enterprise', *National Westminster Bank Quarterly Review* (August 1972).
19 Robson, *Nationalized Industry and Public Ownership*, p. 488.
20 Report of the Labour Party Conference (1973), pp. 166–8.

Chapter VIII

Achievement and Shortfall

This book began by describing the evolution of the welfare state. This penultimate chapter will try to show how far we have achieved welfare objectives and how far we have failed to do so. It is impossible to cover every aspect of the subject in a brief survey, but I hope to provide an appraisal of sufficient scope to enable a broad judgement to be made.

The dictionary meaning of welfare is the state or condition of being well; good fortune; happiness, or well-being; prosperity of a person or community. We can, I think, ignore the idea of happiness from this analysis for the simple reason that happiness is a personal experience which cannot be achieved by collective action, whether of the state or of society, although it can be destroyed by the state. Happiness depends on many imponderable factors which vary with each individual according to his temperament, his biological inheritance, his aspirations, his abilities, his upbringing and the innumerable chances that influence the destiny of every man and woman. As August Heckscher remarks, 'the state cannot make people happy, any more than it can make them wise or good. Public happiness, like private happiness, must be part of the individual.'[1]

Heckscher does not explain what he means by public happiness, although he thinks that the state can do much to foster and define it. He asserts that there is a contradiction between happiness and welfare which has created a basic dilemma for modern liberalism and tends to confuse the relationship between the citizen and the government.[2] The reasons for this alleged contradiction is the tendency to treat welfare as an end in itself, thereby failing to go beyond what he describes as 'the rather dreary, uninspiring concern for social troubles and maladjustments to the accomplishments of the true tasks of a civilised community'.[3] He accuses the welfare worker of believing that discord and conflict can be removed by better housing, social services and a higher standard of living –

only to find that evils such as violence, delinquency and crime continue to exist no matter what improvements are made in such matters.[4]

This criticism is more than a little absurd. Welfare workers are not quite so naive and ignorant as Mr Heckscher supposes; nor is the welfare state concerned only with social services dealing with material conditions. It may be true that the policies of the welfare state began with the relief or prevention of the most obvious evils, such as poverty, squalor, ignorance and unemployment, but they do not stop there. In fact, the concept of welfare can extend to almost every aspect of the well-being of the individual and of society – physical, mental and moral.

The welfare state is not, however, creating a new civilisation, and it was never intended or expected to do so. What gradually emerged as welfare policies evolved was a belief that the political, economic and social aims of the community would be changed or modified; but the culture, the economy, and the political regime would remain substantially unchanged though they were likely to be modified. There neither was nor is a substantial body of opinion in Britain or the other committed welfare states that desires a drastic departure from the civilisation they have inherited, comparable to the communist revolutions in Russia and China.

Mr Heckscher reduces the aim of the welfare state to the provision of a little cash to help men and women face the inevitable vicissitudes of life and to extend institutionalised care to those in need of it. This he thinks is the most society can provide, small though it is. He concedes that almost everything the state has done in these directions can be justified, but considers welfare has the great disadvantage that we become preoccupied with it and lose sight of higher aims and purposes.[5]

It is obvious that if one starts out with a narrow view of the aims and policies of the welfare state, it is not difficult for critics such as August Heckscher to denigrate it on the ground that its aims and policies are narrow! But this is a false view of the welfare state. It is historically true that it has so far been conceived mainly with the pursuit of negative aims such as the relief of poverty, the cure of disease, the overcoming of physical and mental handicaps, the elimination of ignorance and illiteracy, the clearance of slums and the removal of squalor. But those who have contributed most, whether as philosophers or as practical reformers, to the development of the welfare state, have never seen it as limited to negative aims. They have envisaged the welfare state as providing widespread opportunities for the enjoyment and creation of all the many forms of art: drama, literature, ballet, music, painting, poetry, as well as television and radio. They see it aiming at offering the fullest opportunities for individual self-expression through facilities for all kinds of leisure time activities. They see it achieving a much greater degree of participation in the making of political decisions than has so far been attained in this or any other country. Above all, they see it enabling the workpeople to share in the management of economic life and of seeking fuller self-expression in the processes of production. One cannot force people to be creative, but the opportunities for creative self-expression are potentially more ample in the welfare state than in any other kind of polity.

There are, indeed, no limits to the positive aims of the welfare state. This applies particularly to the quality of the environment. No welfare state can be regarded as worthy of the name if its environment is as polluted, noisy, and indifferent to human needs as most large towns, or as ugly as most modern urban development. Until our cities have achieved a high degree of beauty, health, convenience and amenity we shall not have attained environmental welfare, which is an essential aim of the welfare state. With this, of course, goes a high standard of housing, shopping centres, offices and factories, municipal and governmental buildings, theatres, etc. Some of this improvement will depend mainly on private sector activity; some of it mainly or wholly on state policy; some of it on a combination of public and private action. Here again one must distinguish between the welfare state and the welfare society, though bearing in mind that fine public buildings can sometimes set an example which may have a substantial influence on the architecture and style of private construction.

The welfare state embraces the whole nation, not just those members of it who are in need of help. It is a misconception to appraise the welfare state solely in terms of what it has or has not achieved for the poor and underprivileged citizens. The welfare state is properly identified with the public policies of the governmental authorities, and these are distinct from – and sometimes in conflict with – the policies, actions and attitudes of the individuals and groups which form society.

During the past ten or twenty years the vast majority of the British people have been better fed, better clothed, better housed, better educated, better cared for medically, better protected against the vicissitudes of life, and better entertained than at any other time in their history. Much, though not all, of this has been due to state welfare policies. Some of the improvement has been due to the increase of real earnings and the development of the economy.

Many of the advances in the standard of life and the opportunities which are available to the great majority of citizens are a result of public policy. Life in Britain has changed for the better in many respects since 1945. The opening up of higher education to enable almost every young man or woman with the ability and desire to obtain a degree or professional qualification has abolished most of the class privileges formerly attached to higher education. Advertisements for vacancies in industry no longer state 'public schoolboy preferred'. And inside the universities the family background of students is no longer important.

The rise in the level of culture among people of all income groups is a striking phenomenon of recent decades. This is largely due to the work of the BBC in the fields of music, drama and science; and to the Arts Council in the fields of opera, ballet, drama, music, painting, sculpture and poetry. The public libraries have played an important part, and so too have the publishers of paperback books. The living stage is supported out of public funds not only in the West End of London but also in a considerable number of provincial and suburban theatres of quality. There has also been a remarkable growth of good amateur companies throughout the country. Britain has become one of the leading musical centres, and symphony concerts given by subsidised orchestras in London and the main provincial cities attract crowded audiences whose appreciation of music began in school. The building of the Festival Hall by the London County Council has transformed the musical life of the capital.[6]

Public libraries have developed beyond recognition in recent decades. They have contributed to the rising standard of education and to an improvement in public taste. The leading library authorities lend gramophone records and arrange lectures and exhibitions. Our system of public libraries is probably the best in Europe and one of the best in the world. It has driven the private subscription libraries formerly run by Mudies, Boots and The Times Bookclub out of business. The spread of culture in these various ways may well be an influential factor in stimulating public opposition to many of the proposed development schemes whose leading features are often the construction of motorways, faceless office slabs and highrise blocks of flats devoid of architectural interest or aesthetic merit.

A major aim of the welfare state is the abolition of poverty, and this has not been achieved. But the question of whether poverty has even been reduced raises the problem of what is meant by poverty. Poverty on the scale and at the level which existed during the great depression in the 1930s has disappeared, and so too have the pawnshops which enabled so many of the destitute to eke out a precarious existence. But poverty is no longer seen as an absolute condition applicable to everyone living below a specified level of subsistence.[7] It is now perceived as relative to the standard of life prevailing in a society at a given time. Poverty in India has an entirely different meaning from poverty in France, and poverty in Britain today has a different meaning from that which it had in 1910 or 1920. Even within a country a family accustomed to a high income which falls into reduced circumstances might feel poor even though they were still living at a standard which to many people would represent affluence. Disregarding individual distinctions of this kind, poverty which is relative implies that it is no longer possible to define it in terms of the weekly cost of providing a fixed amount of food, clothing and household necessaries in the way which was used by Seebohm Rowntree in his studies of York and those who adopted his method in other towns.

The relativity concept of poverty has been used to point out that the lowest income groups may improve their standard of living without improving their position compared with the rest of the community. When this approach has reached a certain point, poverty in the former sense of the word is replaced by the concept of relative deprivation. The claim of the deprived is then expressed as the need for greater equality. Michael Young has referred to 'lagged equality' as the nearest approach we have achieved in this respect.[8]

It is admittedly not possible to define poverty in absolute terms as though it has a single generally accepted meaning of a permanent kind. A large element of value judgement will inevitably enter into any attempt to formulate a definition; and it may well be useful to have different definitions for different purposes. Relative social or economic deprivation should no doubt be considered as one aspect. But it is going much too far to assert, as Professor Peter Townsend does, that everyone who is not enjoying living conditions and amenities equal to those possessed by the average individual or family in the society of which he is a member is in a state of poverty.[9]

This formulation confuses the question of equality with the question of poverty. In a stratified society such as ours each income group is deprived of some of the living habits, customs, amenities and activities of those in the higher income groups, and the 'average' individual or family is a myth unless it is confined to particular socio-economic classes. In consequence poverty on the Townsend definition will continue until perfect equality is attained throughout society.

The Townsend definition does not correspond with what the great majority of people understand by poverty, namely living below a certain minimum standard of life – a minimum not fixed once and for all, but determined in the light of the resources available to the community.

If poverty is simply identified with inequality, Professor Thomas Wilson points out, neither the growth of the economy nor the policies of the welfare state have made serious inroads on poverty in any country where the relative share of the lower income groups has not increased. 'Many people', he adds, 'would interpret such statements to mean that the standard of living of the poorer families, as measured by the goods and services available to them, had not improved. In this latter sense, "poverty" may well have been reduced and, if so, it is necessary to record this fact without implying for a moment that relative social deprivation is not also important.'[10]

Poverty was formerly regarded as mainly one-dimensional, lack of income being the sole or dominant factor. It is now seen as multi-dimensional. The family suffering from multiple handicaps has now become the object of increasing concern. It is a family in which low wages or unemployment leads to bad housing; this in turn causes poor health and low vitality; these conditions adversely affect the children's performance at school; and this reduces their life prospects when they go out to work. This vicious circle presents a far more complex problem to the public authorities administering welfare services than the mere provision of income maintenance to relieve poverty.

It was for long assumed that the aged formed an overwhelming majority of those living in poverty. Investigations carried out by Professors Abel-Smith and Townsend estimated that in 1960 about two and a quarter million children were living in conditions of poverty, a figure equal to more than two-thirds of the aged poor.[11]

A recent study calculated that about 7 per cent of families and one in eleven children are living in poverty.[12] A substantial proportion of the adult members of these households are in full-time employment. The socially deprived consist of low wage earners, fatherless families, unemployed, disabled, immigrants, and caravan dwellers.[13] Much emphasis has been placed in recent studies of poverty on the importance of family size. One study showed that the proportion of unrelieved poverty was 2 per cent among families with one or two children, but rose to 11 per cent among families with five children and to 20 per cent among larger families.

The burden of poverty falls most heavily on women and on one-parent families. Not only are women's earnings lower than men's, but the social security system discriminates against women except in the one respect of granting them retirement pensions at the age of 60 compared with the age of 65 for men. In 1972, out of 1,912,000 single pensioners on supplementary benefit 1,339,000 were women, and the position today is probably similar.[14]

The report of the Finer Committee on One-Parent Families referred to

'the myth, widely believed in the late 1940s and 1950s, that the welfare state had eradicated poverty. That myth did not survive the statistical and other demonstrations by Titmuss and his fellow workers that the promise of welfare through widening social services had been more impressive than its performance. This rediscovery of poverty led to new definitions and investigations of "the poor", from which it emerged that several millions of British citizens were living in or close to poverty in the affluent society after a long period of full employment and rising real standards for the rest of the population. Among those living in poverty, the fatherless families . . . came to be seen as a distinctive group.'[15]

Apart from the great disability of lacking a male breadwinner is the fact that women are the main source of cheap labour in Britain, as in all other countries. In April 1971 the Committee estimated that there were 620,000 one-parent families containing more than one million children, a figure equal to a tenth of all families with children. About 520,000 of the families were fatherless, owing to separation, divorce, widowhood or because the mother was unmarried. The remaining 100,000 families were motherless.[16]

The Beveridge scheme of national insurance aimed to ensure that 'every citizen, willing to serve according to his powers, has at all times an income sufficient to meet his responsibilities'.[17] The scheme we have established does not achieve this aim nor does it seriously attempt to do so. Three-quarters of all the allowances paid by the Supplementary Benefits Commission go to people in receipt of a pension or other benefit from national insurance. Without the supplementary allowances they would fall below the official poverty line approved each year by Parliament. It is, therefore, the Supplementary Benefits Commission that provides a minimum income intended to relieve or prevent poverty as thus defined.

Of those who claim and receive supplementary benefit, 28 per cent are retirement pensioners, 14 per cent widows, 10 per cent sick and disabled, and 24 per cent unemployed.[18]

The fact that poverty is relieved by means-tested allowances made by the Supplementary Benefits Commission is not necessarily a defect of the British system although it is a departure from the Beveridge scheme. The effectiveness of any given volume of expenditure, Professor Thomas Wilson observes, ought in principle to be increased if the expenditure is made with some regard to need. To have raised the flat rate retirement pension to the level of supplementary benefits would have cost an extra £700m. in 1972, to be met from higher taxation and probably increased social insurance contributions. This would inevitably raise the question of priorities of expenditure. An alternative policy could be to raise the national insurance benefits to the supplementary benefits level without increasing total expenditure under both headings above what it would otherwise have been. The result of this, he concludes, would be to drastically reduce the number of persons below the poverty line, but the poor would be worse off.[19]

An unfortunate aspect of the system is that large numbers of individuals and families are living in poverty because they do not claim benefit to which they are entitled. They comprise people who are either unaware of their rights or unwilling to claim supplementary benefit from a sense of pride or dislike of means-tested benefits. An official inquiry in 1966 estimated that 700,000 families consisting of 850,000 people, amounting to 14 per cent of all retirement pensioners, were in this category. After this startling revelation the National Assistance Board was replaced by the Supplementary Benefits Commission, which conducted a publicity campaign intended to inform people of their rights to benefit. The position has almost certainly been improved but the take-up of supplementary benefits remains low. One estimate suggests that 600,000 old people are still below the poverty line owing to failure to claim.

A second group found to be in a similar position were 35,000 families with two or more children whose father was sick or unemployed. A third group failing to claim consisted of 10,000 fatherless families whose incomes were at least £2 a week below the poverty line. These figures are for 1966 and were contained in an official report based on National Assistance Scales which were lower than those introduced later that year.[20] A fourth group living in poverty are the low-paid workers subject to the wage-stop when unemployed. This precludes the Commission from paying them more when unemployed than they earn when working. In 1971, 24,000 unemployed claimants suffered a reduction of benefit from this cause.[21]

Reduction or refusal of supplementary benefit can arise from other causes. Thus a woman cohabiting with a man who is supporting her cannot lawfully draw supplementary benefit. An unemployed man or woman who is disqualified for receiving unemployment benefit for not more than six weeks by reason of having been dismissed for industrial misconduct, or for having voluntarily left employment without just cause, or for having refused an offer of a suitable job, will have his or her supplementary benefit reduced by 40 per cent. Claimants living in premises in which the rent is unreasonably high or which the Commission think it is unreasonable for them to occupy will have the rent allowance which is normally payable reduced *pro tanto*. This affected 31,760 claimants in 1971.[22] If all these categories are added together the number of households and individuals living below the official poverty line is substantial.

One other point to be noted is that the proportion of persons receiving national insurance benefits who were qualified and willing to claim national assistance or its successor supplementary benefit has increased significantly in recent decades. In the case of those receiving unemployment benefit, it rose from 16 per cent in 1951 to 23 per cent in 1971 and 24 per cent in 1972. In the case of retirement pensioners the proportion rose from 22 per cent in 1951 to 28 per cent in each year from 1969 to 1972. Only sickness or invalidity beneficiaries showed a slight drop from 13 per cent in 1951 and again in 1971 to 11 per cent in 1972.[23]

A separate question is whether the official poverty line has been drawn at an acceptable point, bearing in mind the fact that the definition of poverty involves value judgements on which opinions are likely to differ. The official poverty line, as determined by the scale on which means-tested benefits are provided, has been repeatedly raised. By 1972 it had reached a level almost twice as high in real terms – that is, at constant prices – as it was in 1948, when the new social insurance scheme was launched. In consequence, the poverty line has risen at approximately the same rate as average gross earnings, although there is no formal relation between them. The retirement pensioner has during this period been protected against inflation and also shared in economic growth.[24] Up to the present, therefore, increases in pensions have substantially exceeded the rise in prices. Accelerating inflation will make it difficult to maintain this movement but it will be facilitated by more frequent reviews.

The poverty level in Britain, measured as a proportion of gross average wages, is about 40 per cent, which is about the same as in West Germany, 2 per cent higher than in Belgium, and nearly double what it is in Italy. In France the figure is about 46 per cent.[25] But these percentages do not determine the adequacy of the poverty level in this country because they leave out of account the large differences in gross average wages. If productivity were higher in Britain, if our gross national product had grown at a faster rate, and if, therefore, gross average wages in Britain compared more favourably with those in Germany, France, Sweden, Belgium and other more affluent countries, the poverty line would be higher than it is. Few of the contemporary writers on poverty mention this point.

As already pointed out, it is now widely recognised that poverty is multi-dimensional, with many facets other than the provision of income. Bad housing, homelessness, unemployment, disablement, mental illness, drug addiction, violence, educational failure and other misfortunes or disadvantages are all associated with poverty either as cause or effect, though many of them have ramifications which extend throughout society. Efforts to deal with these problems concern a very wide range of social services, and it is not possible within the scope of this book to attempt an appraisal. So far as the expenditure on these services is concerned, Britain may be allocating a smaller proportion of her gross national product to welfare services than Sweden, West Germany, France, the Netherlands, Belgium and even Italy. But the statistics are of dubious validity and international comparisons may omit many relevant factors.[26] Above all, cost is not the only significant indicator of an effective social service.

We should not ignore or denigrate the large advances that have been made since 1945 in social security, health, housing, education, recreation and many other services, despite the unsolved problems of dealing with poverty.

Some commentators argue that poverty is the result of the class structure of British society, and contend that this can only be destroyed by a socialist revolution.[27] I do not share this view. It is indisputable that there is substantially less poverty today than during the inter-war years, and it is highly probable that the condition of the poor will continue to be improved during the coming years.

Even with these reservations it would be foolish to claim that the British welfare state has succeeded in maximising welfare and minimising hardship, poverty, squalor, ignorance and disease. The efforts of the past thirty years show a picture of achievement in some directions and shortfall in others.

Some of the deficiencies or defects are due to sheer ignorance about how to deal effectively with certain types of problem families or with people suffering from various physical, mental or moral handicaps which cause them to become drop-outs or lay-abouts or drug addicts or hooligans or thieves or rapists or irresponsible parents. Some of them are due to lack of human resources, such as social workers, psychiatrists and psychologists. Some of them are due to financial shortages resulting from the poor performance of the economy. Some of them are due to indifference or apathy on the part of governments, or to the budgetary priorities of Chancellors of the Exchequer and the Cabinet. Some of them are due to the incompetence or neglect of parents, the failure of teachers, or the limited knowledge of the medical profession. Some of them may be due, as Richard Titmuss suggested, to the fact that the welfare state is not helping those whose need is greatest but is benefiting most those who may need it least.[28] Some may be due to an increasing part of the cost of services in kind going to those who administer the welfare services rather than to those who should benefit by the services, or to providing a higher standard of service for the symptoms of need rather than to curing or preventing its causes.[29] Whatever the reasons, until these deficiences are remedied, there will remain large areas of poverty, avoidable ill health, homelessness, unemployment, unemployability, deprivation, violence, vandalism, cruelty and misery.

In recent years numerous books, pamphlets and articles have appeared denouncing the degree of social and economic inequality which now exists, criticising Labour governments for having done little to rectify the position, accusing Conservative governments for having increased inequality, and calling for drastic measures of reform.[30] Some writers declare that poverty cannot be abolished without equality being established. Mr J. C. Kincaid, a lecturer in social policy at Leeds University, alleges that there is widespread poverty resulting from the limited effectiveness of the social security system. He contends that radical improvements in social security provision are urgently needed and long overdue in Britain. He argues that an adequate system cannot be created without a substantial redistribution of income, for some are rich because some are poor; and the tax system is itself an important cause of poverty. He sees no hope for any appreciable improvement in social security provision without a socialist revolution; and in order to achieve this he urges the creation of a political party of revolutionary socialists to sweep away the capitalist system and establish social and economic equality.[31]

This approach is typical of a number of writers on social administration in Britain at the present time, though not many of them go to such extreme lengths as Mr Kincaid. It is worth considering briefly the assumptions underlying his theme. First, he assumes that poverty cannot be abolished in a capitalist society or one with a mixed economy. He does not inquire why or how this has in fact been achieved in Sweden or New Zealand, both of which are welfare states, relying mainly on private enterprise. Second, he omits any consideration of the state of the economy, the size of the GNP, or the effect on production of the massive redistribution he recommends. He assumes that everything else in the economy will remain unchanged while he redistributes the product on a vast scale. Third, like many of those who share this approach, he shows no interest in the standard of living of the great majority of the nation who do not fall below the poverty line.

The elimination of genuine poverty is an essential aim of the welfare state, and any country which has the means to achieve this aim but has not done so has failed in a major respect as a welfare state. To the extent that poverty still exists in Britain, we have not fulfilled the aspirations of a welfare state. In this context poverty should be taken to mean lack of access to a standard of life which provides the essentials for the maintenance of bodily and mental health, together with reasonable opportunities for family life and the upbringing of children – but not more than that.

Equality is generally regarded as a fundamental aim of socialism, though there is gross inequality in the Soviet Union and the other communist states in Eastern Europe. But it cannot be classed as a basic element in the welfare state, for the simple reason that it has not been demonstrated, nor is it widely believed, that the welfare of the whole society would be increased if equality were imposed upon it. Even if poverty could be eliminated by the transfer of resources from the better off to the poor – and this is an unproved assertion – the welfare of everyone else would be decreased, not just in economic terms but in terms of the loss of freedom. Neither Mr Kincaid nor other writers have shown that poverty cannot be abolished within the welfare state. Already a vast amount of the poverty that existed between the two World Wars has been abolished and I believe most of the remainder, as defined above, could be abolished, without a revolutionary change in our society, if a serious effort were made to do so.

Quite apart from the question of poverty, increasing interest has been shown in recent years in the subject of equality. Socialism in Britain was traditionally founded on the principle of replacing capitalism by various forms of public or social ownership, such as nationalisation, municipal trading and consumers' co-operation. A shift of emphasis began when the late Hugh Gaitskell declared, as leader of the Parliamentary Labour Party, that 'Socialism is about equality', and subsequently tried in vain to secure the elimination from the aims of the Labour Party of clause 4, which calls for common ownership of the means of production and their popular administration and control.

The extent to which the policies of the welfare state have redistributed wealth and income is severely contested among economists who have studied the available evidence. The leading protagonists include Professor A. B. Atkinson, who has reviewed the very limited statistical evidence bearing on the subject. His chief conclusion is that redistribution has mainly been from the very rich to the rich.[32]

Mr George Polanyi and Mr John B. Wood vigorously oppose this view and criticise the use of the estate duty statistics on which it is founded. They even believe that the statistical approach is questionable when it contradicts the visible signs of an all-round improvement in the standard of living in terms of much wider ownership of cars, television sets, household durables, fuel consumption, holidays abroad, the consumption of wine, and so forth. They present conflicting evidence to show that redistribution has been far greater than Professor Atkinson alleged. Professor Atkinson concedes that the estimates of individual wealth-holding among the living which are based on estate duty information about deceased persons who possessed estates liable to tax tend to exaggerate the degree to which wealth is concentrated. He does not agree with the Polyani–Wood suggestion that the inequalities disclosed by the Inland Revenue figures are largely explained by the age composition of those whose estates are taxed after death, since these include a lifetime's earnings and saving.

There are many interesting aspects of this discussion concerning the validity of the inferences which can be drawn from the statistics, the definition of wealth, the amount and distribution of 'missing' wealth, the several ways in which bias is introduced into the figures, and the question of including national insurance rights and a share in the nationalised industries in the valuation of individual wealth and its distribution.

Some of the difficulties in discovering the true distribution of wealth are due to the imperfect statistics and other information which is available. But some of the difficulties arise from fundamental disagreements about the concept of wealth. Mr W. G. Runciman, for example, drew attention to numerous items not included by Professor Atkinson in his estimates of wealth. They included human capital in education and training, credit facilities, the assets of trade unions, and money distributed by charities.[33]

It is not my intention to participate in the technicalities of this debate, far less to pronounce on the divergent views of the disputants. Professor Atkinson recognises that the statistics on which his conclusions are based are unsatisfactory from many points of view, but he believes that after adjusting them in various ways the general dimensions in the distribution of wealth can be discerned, and these show gross inequalities which he wishes to modify.

We may hope that the Royal Commission which is inquiring into this subject will succeed in obtaining accurate information about the distribution of income and wealth among the people of Britain which will provide a more satisfactory factual basis for discussion than at present exists.

Meanwhile, it is possible to make three observations on the subject. One is that the fiscal system which prevailed until 1974 was highly unsatisfactory because it combined very high rates of estate duty on the transfer of wealth at death with almost unlimited opportunities for avoiding taxation by gifts made more than seven years before death and other means widely used by the wealthy. This wide open door to avoidance has perpetuated the acquisition of great wealth by inheritance. It has now been closed.

In the second place, the fiscal system has done nothing to encourage redistribution of wealth by the division of estates. As the liability to death duty falls on a deceased person's estate there is no incentive for him or her to divide it among several persons. If the tax were to fall on those inheriting wealth in a steeply graduated scale covering all the bequests received during a person's lifetime, a testator would have a strong incentive to divide a large estate among several beneficiaries in order to reduce the total liability to tax.

Thirdly, whatever may be the trend in the distribution of wealth in Britain, it is well known that there are some immensely wealthy families whose fortunes are derived wholly or mainly from inheritance. These individuals are seldom found among the dynamic leaders of industry, commerce or finance. They are not prominent in the arts or in science. They are not renowned for their philanthropic works: indeed, the meanness of the owners of great inherited fortunes in Britain is in strong contrast to the generosity of wealthy Americans. One can reasonably conclude that the inheritance of great wealth is not generally conducive to the welfare of the individuals who possess it or to that of the nation.

The proposals for reform advocated by Professor Atkinson appear well designed to fulfil the purposes of a welfare state. He advocates the replacement of estate duty by a capital receipts tax. This would be a tax levied at a steeply progressive rate on the total of bequests and gifts received by a beneficiary during his lifetime. The effect would be to reduce the amount of tax falling on a large estate the more widely it were distributed. He advocates this as an alternative to an annual wealth tax on the ground that it distinguishes between inherited wealth and the savings which have been earned by a man during his lifetime. Since earning and saving are of great benefit to the economy, the virtue of this reform is that they would not be discouraged.[34]

Professor Sandford, a leading economist on taxation, shares the view that if the main purpose is to reduce inequalities, an inheritance tax would be far more effective than estate duty. He emphasises that it is the large bequests rather than large estates which perpetuate inequality.[35]

All welfare states have mixed economies, and this should be recognised as a necessary and desirable feature. A mixed economy is likely to be able to safeguard the freedom of choice of both producer and consumer and prevent the oppression that exists when both economic and political power are concentrated in the hands of the state, or if vast capitalist empires dominate the economic and the political arena. If private enterprise forms a substantial part of the economy in a welfare state, this will set limits to the degree of equality which can be achieved, for capitalism generates inequality in any society in which it operates successfully. The welfare state can and should be continually reducing extreme inequalities by progressive taxation and by social services; and it should actively promote a rising level of equal opportunity. It should provide a minimum standard of life for all, and fix a ceiling to the wealth any individual can inherit but not to the wealth he can earn. It can carry out several other measures to reduce poverty and assist the underprivileged. But in the final analysis the pursuit of equality as an end in itself marks a clear line of demarcation between the aims of the welfare state and the objectives of socialism.

Social policy has had a profound effect on the lives and prospects of both the old and the young. The material needs of the aged have been borne in mind by every government, partly because they are an important sector of the electorate, and partly out of humanitarian motives. In consequence, sheer destitution among the old has almost disappeared. The National Health Service and geriatric care have led to an extension of life among those who have lost some or most of their faculties. It has been truly remarked that our society has gained longevity but has not yet found out what to do with it.[36]

Parallel with this provision has been a rigid insistence on retirement from employment at a fixed age regardless of the physical or mental capacity of the individual. Doctors in the health service and civil servants must retire at the age of 60, in common with that prescribed by many private and public undertakings. Compulsory retirement at a fixed age from employment can be very cruel in its consequences at all levels. Many of the 65-year-olds, remarks Piet Thoenes, are still far too fit to be doing nothing.[37] A growing section of the population is being forced into involuntary unemployment, which in consequence imposes an increased burden on the workforce. Professor Dahrendorf deplores the cruelty and waste of compelling people to sever all the ties binding them to their jobs when the day arrives for instant retirement.[38]

Mr Enoch Powell, in his reflections on the welfare state, wrote that the problem of providing for the old is not primarily a financial one, but of how the necessary support, in a physical and environmental sense, can be available to millions of ageing individuals in a modern industrial society. He remarked on the lack of purpose in the provision for old age, an absence of common values which could give it meaning.[39] A significant purpose would have to take account of the loneliness of many old persons in a society in which the nuclear family prevails, and the lack of function, status and interest caused by compulsory retirement. This is a problem which concerns society and not merely the state.

At the other end of the scale, more has been done for the young than at any other period of history. This applies not only to the continual expansion and development of the system of public education, the care of deprived or ill-treated children, restrictions on the employment or exploitation of children, but also to the help given to young people to find congenial and promising careers. They have recently been given the right to vote at the age of 18, and several other rights and obligations have been conferred on them by the state. These measures have immensely widened the opportunities available to young people whose parents lack influence or wealth. The young are, indeed, among those who have benefited most from the welfare state.

A contemporaneous movement has been the influence in Britain of the American cult of youth, which can be observed in many walks of life. One unfortunate result of this is the displacement of men aged between 40 and 45 as the most sought-after candidates for executive positions in industry and commerce in favour of those in the 28 to 35 age group.

The late Karl Mannheim expressed the view that the specific function of youth is as a revitalising agent which comes to the fore when a society needs to adjust quickly to rapidly changing or completely new circumstances.[40] The cult of youth is less the result of state policy than of an attitude pervading society. Many observers doubt whether it has enabled British society to adjust, or to adjust quickly enough, to the immense changes in the economic, political and international position that the United Kingdom has undergone since the end of the Second World War. The excessive conservatism in industry and commerce, the unyielding traditionalism in management practices, the old-fashioned organisation and out-of-date policies of the trade unions, their narrow-minded nationalism, have often been identified as prime causes of the country's industrial decline and slow rate of economic growth.

This view was borne out by the appraisal of a group of leading American and Canadian economists who wrote a report entitled *Britain's Economic Prospects* after conducting detailed research. The final chapter advocated raising economic efficiency mainly because more rapid growth would create a greater capacity to adapt and reallocate. Yet the concluding paragraph asked, 'Are we not propounding growth and change in a society where don and docker alike prefer tradition, leisure and stability? This may be. But many segments of British society have declared for growth, or at least for the fruits of growth . . .'[41] This appraisal of the conservatism that prevails in industry in no way precludes the rapid and continual changes in fashion, manners, modes of address, eating habits, clothes, hair styles, relations between men and women, and between parents and children, etc., referred to in an earlier chapter.[42]

The influence of the young has been considerable in upholding the rights of the underprivileged, the old and helpless, and coloured immigrants. Students in particular have been the declared opponents of racialism in all its forms and in so doing have assisted welfare state policies on race relations. The more articulate sections of the younger age groups have often been anti-Establishment. The weakness of this aspect of the youth movement is that it has been, and still is, mainly negative in its aims; so that while student and other groups have expressed opposition to a great many policies, actions and regimes, it is difficult to discover what are their positive goals, if any.

The Provo movement[43] in the Netherlands showed that the dislike and rejection of the consumer society by many of the younger generation could lead to drastic changes if it were formulated in terms of practical alternatives. The consumer society is one in which the main emphasis is placed on consumption as the principal value in life, and production is seen only as a prelude to consumption. Work is regarded merely as a means to a higher standard of living, and the worker is concerned with little except his pecuniary reward and the forms of consumption which it brings within his reach.[44]

The amount and scope of freedom must occupy a major place in any appraisal of the welfare state or welfare society. Many changes have taken place in this sphere during the past thirty years. In the eighteenth and nineteenth centuries freedom was achieved by asserting and defending the rights of the individual against interference by the state. This was the essential aim of the *laissez-faire* state. In recent decades many kinds of freedom have been obtained by the individual through the activities of the state. The most important of these freedoms is the enlarged opportunity which the system of public education provides to enable young people to enter any occupation for which their abilities fit them, if they are prepared to acquire the necessary qualifications. The National Health Service provides freedom of a different kind. It enables men, women and children to receive a full range of medical treatment and thereby to attain improved health or help to overcome physical handicaps. Social insurance and supplementary benefits give a certain measure of freedom, though not a large one, from the financial anxieties and hardships caused by unemployment, sickness, accidents, invalidity, retirement and widowhood.

A wide range of liberties has been introduced into British society by legislation dealing with sex, marital relations, and family responsibilities. These include freedom to obtain a divorce when

a marriage has broken down without any longer having to prove
a matrimonial offence; freedom for adult consenting males to
satisfy their homosexual desires in private without committing a
crime; freedom accorded to pregnant women to obtain an abortion
if certain conditions are satisfied. Beyond these public policies are
the widespread sexual freedoms which are not the result of legislation but of a change in social attitudes and moral values affecting
all classes and all ages of men and women. The critics of these
libertarian policies deny that they are attributes of the welfare
state or even of welfare. But this is a mistaken view. The permissive
society is in fact part of the welfare state, although freedom in
these spheres can be abused as can all other forms of freedom.

In some spheres the welfare state has curtailed freedom in the
general interest. Thus, in the economic sphere freedom has been
restricted to prevent the creation of monopolistic firms or practices
which could be detrimental to consumers. Retail price fixing by
manufacturers has been forbidden; and the law requires the weight
and contents of food and drugs to be stated on the package. All
such controls, which aim at protecting the consumer, can be
classified as welfare measures.

Many controls regulate conduct in ways that involve a reduction
of freedom for some people and an increase of freedom for others.
A person may not drive a motorcar unless it is insured against
third party risks, and the licensing law requires it to be examined
at regular intervals to ensure that it is fit for the road. Thus people
are prevented from driving cars in a dangerous condition and
causing injury to other persons or property for which they might
be unable to pay compensation. But this reduction of freedom of
some persons enlarges the freedom of others by saving them from
these particular risks.

A similar situation exists in regard to the control of land use.
It is a substantial reduction of freedom for the owner when he
cannot develop his land as he wishes or when a manufacturer is
not permitted to locate his factory where he chooses or a developer
to build an office block on the site or even in the town of his choice.
But town and country planning is unquestionably a welfare function,
and although no one would claim that every plan or development
control is the best possible one in the circumstances, the general
results of town and country planning in Britain are immeasurably
better than those which would have occurred if it had not existed.
The need to control the use of land in the interests of the community is so essential in the welfare state that it overrides the
freedom of a landowner to do what he pleases with his land.

As a broad generalisation, we can say that whereas welfare state policies have a strong tendency to enlarge personal freedom, they tend to curtail the freedom of individuals to dispose of their property as they choose.

Some observers think that the freedom we have already gained has led to many of the maladies from which our society suffers. J. A. C. Brown remarks that in achieving freedom from the bonds of tradition, family ties, and accustomed habits and duties, we have not simply promoted a high degree of individualisation, but also severed all ties between one individual and another and isolated each one from his fellow men. In this isolation, he declares, we shall find 'many of the answers to the problems of industrial unrest, increasing neurosis and crime, the pervading sense of help- lessness, and lack of meaning in the lives of many people today'.[45] That there is a lack of solidarity in our society cannot be denied. The consensus of the Second World War and the early post-war years has disappeared, and unity is seldom apparent except when an external threat, such as the conflict in Northern Ireland, or senseless violence to innocent persons is caused by alien hands. It is obvious that unlimited freedom is incompatible with the welfare state or any other kind of state. What is less obvious is the nature and degree of freedom which is likely to maximise welfare. There is a long tradition in Britain which is strongly in favour of freedom of an undifferentiated kind, but there are signs that some concepts of freedom are threatening the welfare state and the welfare society.

An outstanding example is the constant disruption of production by strikes, whether 'official' or 'unofficial', arising from the freedom of every group of workers to stop work if they or their shop stewards are dissatisfied not only with wages or conditions of employment, but with almost any decision or action of the manage- ment or of their fellow workers or of a rival trade union with which they disagree. This belief in unlimited industrial freedom to strike has spread from private enterprise to publicly owned industries, the Civil Service, local government officers, school teachers, members of the medical professions and others.

In the background looms an even more insidious threat. The central dilemma of our time is the fact that every organisation looks to the government of the day to solve its problems, while at the same time withholding recognition of its authority, acceptance of its decisions, and support for its policies, which are necessary if government is to solve many of these problems. There is, in fact, a decline of authority which affects both central and local govern- ment, the police, the courts of law, industrial management, trade union leaders, school teachers, the clergy, and parents. We are accustomed to make glib contrasts between 'democratic' and 'authoritarian' regimes; but without possessing adequate authority a democratic government may find it impossible to put welfare policies into effect. To say this does not imply that the creed of the authoritarian [46] should prevail, but it does mean that unless the government of a welfare state is accorded a sufficient degree of support and obedience, it cannot operate effectively. Future development of the welfare state is likely to be severely handicapped by the decline of authority from which all British governments now suffer.

Sir Geoffrey Vickers detects a mounting degree of alienation between people in their personal capacities and *all* the institutions on which they depend – not just the government. This he considers a natural attitude among people who have lost confidence in traditional standards of distributing wealth, and in the justice of the market, and who distrust the immense and growing powers of institutions and the officials who run them.[47] Whether natural or not, this attitude is highly dangerous to the integrity not only of the state, but of society. Neither can hope to operate successfully if large numbers of persons have lost faith in the political, social and economic institutions which bind together the millions of individuals who form the state. This disillusion may be partly due to the increasing size of organisations. The creation of giant government departments, large local authorities, huge public corporations, merged industrial and commercial firms, bigger trade unions, multinational corporations, are among the commonest phenomena of our time; and the larger the organisation, the more remote the individual feels from the centre where policy is made.

The removal of discrimination against women in the social and economic spheres is essential not only to the welfare state but also to a welfare society. Legislation and governmental action can compel employers to pay women the same wages or salaries as men; they cannot compel employers to employ women. Government can insist that women shall be eligible for the highest posts in the Civil Service; but that will not ensure that more than a handful of women will obtain those posts. The legal profession, the medical profession, the House of Commons, and ministerial posts, have all been open to women for many years, yet the proportion of women in those occupations is very small. The Conservative and Labour Parties profess to be champions of women's economic and social rights, but neither of them have had more than one woman in the Cabinet. Throughout British society there is strong resistance, even opposition, to giving women equal rights in practice. There is therefore a wide gulf between the welfare state and the welfare society in this matter.

Welfare policies of great potential value are those that aim at assisting the most depressed urban areas to remedy some of their handicaps. There are three such policies at the present time. In 1967 the Plowden Report drew attention to the close relation between home and school. It pointed to the handicaps which children living in deprived areas suffer because their home background gives no encouragement or support for their learning. The report recommended a policy of positive discrimination in favour of such areas, which would improve the schools physically and raise the level of teaching in them in order to assist the children to overcome their home handicaps. This led shortly afterwards to the Department of Education and Science designating a number of Educational Priority Areas, in which teachers in schools of exceptional difficulty would receive a special allowance. Funds would be provided for building new primary schools, and, somewhat later, for a programme for setting up nursery education.

A broader response[48] to the needs of areas of multiple deprivation was embodied in the Urban Aid Programme launched by the Labour Government in 1968 to provide further help in housing, education and health to a number of cities and large towns where existing services were under strain. These came to be known as urban areas of special social need. An Act[49] was passed soon afterwards enabling the Home Secretary to make grants to local authorities who incur expenditure by reason of the existence in any urban area of special social need. These grants amount to 75 per cent of the cost of a scheme and may extend for a period of five years. The Department of Health and Social Security and the Department of the Environment were also involved. The Urban Aid Programme was largely due to the Seebohm Committee on Local Authority and Allied Personal Social Services,[50] whose report recommended the designation of areas of special need which should receive additional resources to carry out comprehensive schemes in co-operation with existing services concerned with health, education, housing and other social needs.

Areas of special need have not been defined. They are areas of urban deprivation suffering from poor living conditions or acute social problems, such as deficiencies in the physical environment, dilapidated housing, overcrowding, large families, juvenile delinquency, inadequate community services, mental disorder, children in care – all at rates higher than the average.

The Community Development Project is in many respects similar in aim to the Urban Aid Programme: its object is to relieve acute social need and thereby to improve the quality of life of those living in deprived areas. The principal difference is that it relies on self-help rather than on the statutory welfare services. It is hoped that community leaders will provide some of the initiative and ideas which are needed to improve the standard of living in their areas.

Substantial but not enormous sums have been allocated to these programmes during the past few years. They have provided nursery schools and classes, day nurseries, adventure playgrounds, community centres, and centres for giving advice on family matters, on housing and on legal questions. Family planning services, literary and language classes, playgroups, the services of community workers and other items have been financed from this source.

A more comprehensive strategy was announced in July 1974 by Mr Jenkins, the Home Secretary. This aims at bringing about, through the co-ordinated efforts of central and local authorities, the National Health Service, regional water boards, vountary bodies and residents, a revision of priorities in favour of the people living in the most deprived areas. Local authorities will be asked to prepare comprehensive community programmes for such areas. The programmes will identify the entire range of economic, social, physical and environmental problems from which each area is suffering, and the remedies proposed to overcome them.

Policies such as these, aiming at positive discrimination in favour of underprivileged areas, are significant for several reasons. First, they move from a concern with individual families or individuals suffering from multiple handicaps to a policy of discrimination in favour of whole areas adversely affected by inferior social, economic and environmental conditions. Second, they attempt to concentrate the resources and powers of central and local authorities, voluntary bodies, and the energies and leadership of members of the local community, in a concerted effort to bring about a comprehensive improvement. Third, the narrow departmental outlook has been abandoned both at central and local levels. Fourth, research teams have been appointed which it is hoped will throw light on the nature and origin of the maladies afflicting the selected areas, define their characteristics, and help to prescribe the remedies. Despite their limitations the schemes are of great potential value.[51] They represent a new and significant type of approach valuable alike for the welfare state and the welfare society.

The negative aims of the welfare state relate to traditional tasks such as reducing poverty, clearing slums, housing the homeless, educating the illiterate, curing the sick, assisting the handicapped, protecting neglected or ill-treated children and caring for the aged. We have made considerable progress in nearly all these spheres during the past thirty years, although this is not generally realised because standards have risen and much more information is available about some of them than formerly. Immense efforts will be required if further substantial advances are to be made in overcoming these defects.

Meanwhile, we are confronted by growth in the number of drug addicts,[52] especially among the young; by an increased incidence of venereal disease,[53] mental illness and mental handicap.[54] We have become acutely aware of the need to deal with baby battering, wife beating, hooliganism, vandalism, alcoholism, and other symptoms of human frustration, anger or misery which did not figure in the programmes of social reformers twenty-five or thirty years ago. We have much more information about these phenomena than in the past but little knowledge of their causes or how to prevent them. Whether they are due to social causes or to individual physical, moral and mental defects, or a mixture of both, is not known. But their existence on a substantial scale indicates shortcomings in the performances of the welfare state and the welfare society. The need to overcome such evils must be included among the negative aims of the welfare state.

When, however, we consider the positive goals of the welfare state it is much more difficult to know in which directions we should move and what policies we should adopt.

Should we, for example, aim at a more contented society in our search for welfare? And if so, what are the present causes of discontent? How far is contentment compatible with the vast apparatus of publicity and sales promotion which makes people dissatisfied with last year's fashions or motorcars in order to sell them this year's models? Do people on the whole gain or lose in satisfaction from the competitive struggle to keep up with, or rather to keep ahead of, the Joneses? Should we aim at a more adventurous society rather than a more contented one? Does a system which tries to protect individuals from the vicissitudes of life tend to make people too cautious in their approach to problems needing boldness rather than excessive prudence? Does the welfare state foster qualities of initiative and courage, and the willingness to take risks, which are necessary for achievement in many fields of endeavour? And if not, how can we correct this tendency without abandoning social security? Is the national addiction to gambling due to a subconscious desire to compensate for the social security we have so laboriously constructed, and must certainly retain and improve?

It is by no means clear what degree of equality will produce the most favourable conditions for welfare; nor how much equality the British people really desire or will accept. The answer to this crucial question should have regard both to the past and to the future. Hitherto, the remarkable contributions which this country has made to parliamentary government, science, medicine, navigation, aeronautics, literature, drama, poetry, technology and other areas of human achievement have been due to the exceptional exertions of exceptional men. If we are to continue to make great contributions we must recognise that the attainment of a high standard of welfare for the common man is no substitute for the exceptional achievements of the uncommon individual. Our aim should therefore be to bring about conditions which, while ensuring a relatively high general level of welfare, will be such as to evoke the exceptional efforts of men and women of outstanding ability. We can undoubtedly increase greatly the number of those who are able to make a creative contribution to civilised life, but only if we make the development of exceptional ability an important part of public policy, especially in the sphere of education. If we are not willing to cultivate and reward exceptional talent, on the ground that to do so offends against the principle of equality, both we and the world will suffer from this attitude.

If this statement is denounced as elitism, so be it. The denouncement does not affect its truth. What is important is that there are signs that the contemporary obsession with equality as the sole road to Utopia is already threatening centres of excellence in education and medicine which one would normally expect to be the training grounds for a considerable proportion of men and women of exceptional ability.

At the secondary education level the basic inequalities have been the division of the state schools into grammar schools, technical schools, and secondary modern. These three categories were intended to cater respectively for the academically brightest children, those with technical abilities, and the residue. The separation was carried out by means of the discredited eleven-plus examination which classified the children according to their abilities. This tripartite system was criticised and later opposed by the Labour Party mainly on social and ideological grounds, and the comprehensive school was advocated because it appeared to conform to the principle of egalitarianism. The views of people professionally concerned with secondary education were subordinated to the ideological argument. This led to the introduction of the comprehensive school as the only type which a Labour Minister of Education would approve for new construction, and increasing pressure has been placed on local education authorities to 'go comprehensive'. Some years passed before it was realised that streaming within the comprehensive school had replaced external streaming in the tripartite system.[55]

The most difficult problem facing the protagonists of educational egalitarianism is the existence of the public schools which, with the private preparatory schools from which most of their pupils come, form virtually a separate sector of primary and secondary education. Public school boys and girls grow up and are educated in a different world from those who attend the state schools. There are obvious disadvantages to society in having a public and a private system of education, since it results in children attending different schools according to the wealth of their parents. They may meet at the university but it will be as strangers.

On the other hand, the leading public schools are the best secondary schools in the country. They have larger resources, better premises and grounds, can attract excellent teachers, have a low pupil–teacher ratio, are better equipped with workshops and laboratories, and have good academic traditions. Those at the lower end of the list are much weaker. Many of the preparatory schools have been fighting against adverse conditions and are facing severe difficulties.

Because of their quality, history and traditions, the public schools could not be closed or destroyed. If an attempt were made to do so, there would be a violent protest and the parents concerned would doubtless send their children to schools in other countries rather than be compelled to send them to the municipal schools. Moreover, there is a need for more boarding schools, not fewer, and the municipal schools are day schools.

The Labour Party's proposal is, therefore, that the public schools shall be integrated in the national system of education. A Commission was appointed by Mr Crosland (and continued by Mr Short who succeeded him as Secretary of State for Education and Science) whose terms of reference explicitly required them to advise on this question as their main function. The Commission was expected to pay attention to the creation of a socially mixed entry into the schools and also to move towards a progressively wider range of academic attainment among public school pupils, so that the public school sector would increasingly conform with the national policy for the maintained sector.

The Commission carried out its task faithfully by defining several possible roles and methods of integration which could be envisaged. An essential feature of them all would be the requirement that not less than half the pupils would be grant-aided and would come from municipal maintained schools. This could have beneficial results from a social point of view, but it could be academically damaging by lowering the entrance requirements. The Commission was aware of this but brushed it aside without seriously considering the consequences.

'Whatever course we recommend', declared the report, 'must be practical, and this is why we shall propose that the schools should accept children of lower ability than many of them are accustomed to accept and should modify their curriculum, but without becoming fully comprehensive. If this were done, the independent schools could help to provide places for a large proportion of children who need to go to a boarding school; and these schools would become less socially divisive.'[56]

The Commission dismissed the fear that the scheme would lead to the creation of a new 'snob sector' of semi-independent boarding and day schools which would attract the brightest pupils from the comprehensives. 'Nor do we think that the academic standards of the independent [i.e. public] schools would be destroyed by admitting boys and girls who are less advanced than their contemporaries who got a better start in life.'[57] The basis for this complacent statement was the belief that children of lower social classes may appear to be less intelligent on entering secondary school, but given the right opportunities many of them catch up by the time they leave school. Moreover, they expressed the view that 'the academic traditions of the public schools are not likely to be destroyed by accepting such children'.[58] The use of the word 'destroyed' twice in this context is notable, for by using it the Commission side-stepped the real issue, which is whether the scheme they recommended would *lower* the academic standards and academic traditions of the public schools.

The Public Schools Commission believed they were pursuing a valuable philosophy of education, the origins of which went back to the Crowther Report on secondary education which suggested that the supply of talent might be enlarged. That report said there was a grave waste of talent through too early an abandonment of formal education. This was to be found mainly in the middle range between the brightest quarter and the great mass of ordinary children. The Newsom Report, *Half our Future,* thought that the supply of talent could be increased with proper education. The Public Schools Commission were also influenced by the Plowden Report which recommended additional resources to improve the primary education available for the underprivileged, especially the less able pupils.[59]

None of these theories about the less able or the early leavers or the submerged pupils has any bearing on the supremely important question of how best to provide for the exceptionally gifted children.

It was on this issue that the Public Schools Commission divided, although all of them signed the report. A majority wanted children possessing exceptional gifts of an academic kind to be educated with other children in a comprehensive system, supplemented by additional courses, attendance at special centres or classes outside normal school hours; while a minority wished to preserve and develop some highly selective schools taking children of normal secondary age comprising about the top 2 per cent of the ability range. These schools could be evolved from any sector of the educational system and would charge no fees.

All the members of the Commission agreed that further research and experiment is necessary to ensure that the talents of the exceptionally gifted pupils are not wasted.[60] Yet despite the admission that little is known about the way in which the exceptional gifts of the most talented children can best be nurtured and developed, most of the Commissioners were prepared to gamble with this priceless national asset by so lowering the standards of entry into the public schools that the best of them might cease to be centres of excellence within a few years. The minority foresaw that this could happen if the exceptionally able pupils were dispersed through the comprehensive system. They will tend to grow bored and to fall back, to under-achieve and to fail even to stimulate other children in the way that is expected of them. To cultivate exceptional talent, they insisted, the ablest pupils and teachers must both be concentrated in schools of a special kind.[61]

The attack on direct grant schools may turn out to be equally damaging to the best of them, which are also centres of excellence. They are at present receiving grants amounting to £13m on condition they accept not less than a quarter of their pupils from maintained schools without charging fees for them. The Public Schools Commission were impressed by their academic achievements: 60 per cent of the pupils stay at school till 18 years of age; 62 per cent of boys and 50 per cent of girls get two or more A levels; and 75 per cent go on to some kind of full-time further education; 38 per cent to a university.[62] The Labour Government has announced its intention of stopping the grant, thereby giving the schools the alternative of becoming ordinary maintained comprehensives or becoming entirely independent. Their financial position as independent schools will undoubtedly be gravely threatened at a later stage by the threat to remove any fiscal advantages they enjoy as charities.

The impetus behind Labour's drive for comprehensive schools, its dislike of streaming, the abolition of grammar schools, the hostility to direct grant and public schools, has been the ideological doctrine of equality. The Conservative opposition to these policies has also been politically motivated. The Black Paper on *The Crisis in Education*[63] tried to argue in educational terms for excellence and elitism but the response by Mr Short, when Secretary of State for Education, was on political grounds. Those who believe first and foremost in egalitarianism appear to believe that raising the general level of education cannot or should not be accompanied by the exceptional treatment of children of exceptional ability. In their view elitism, even when based on innate ability, is incompatible with social equality and therefore unacceptable. They consider equality of opportunity as insufficient to satisfy their desire for absolute equality.

The role of education in cultivating intellectual abilities has not been of much importance in the discussions at the political and parliamentary level, though it occupied a prominent place in the Black Paper essays. On this question Professor Marshall remarks: 'Competitive selection through the educational system must remain with us to a considerable extent. The welfare state is bound to pick the children of high ability for higher education and for higher jobs, and to do this with the interests of the community as well as the rights of the children in mind. But the more use it can at the same time make of allocation to courses suited to special tastes and abilities the better.'[64] He thinks the welfare state is in danger of tying itself in knots in an attempt to do things which are self-contradictory, of which the competitive selection of children according to their ability while at the same time maintaining a strict egalitarianism in the schools is one example. The insistence on parity of esteem of a kind which denies differences in the levels of ability required for different types of education and different kinds of teaching is another example.

The emphasis on social equality as the supreme aim of the

education system could lead to an anti-intellectualism in the schools which might have very serious long-term effects in lowering the potential intellectual contribution of a whole generation of adults. The strongest arguments in the Black Paper were those designed to show that the unstreamed comprehensive schools had resulted in a lowering of intellectual standards in those schools.[65]

A different situation exists in the health service. The great majority of middle- and upper-middle-class patients use the National Health Service, although most general practitioners and a high proportion of consultants take private patients. The Labour Party and the trade unions representing the ancillary workers in the hospitals are opposed to the provision of private beds in public hospitals, and object to consultants using the resources of the hospitals to examine and treat private patients, who pay fees to the physicians and surgeons and high charges to the hospitals for accommodation, nursing and the so-called hotel services. Some trade unions ordered their members to refuse to provide services for private patients in NHS hospitals in 1974 and 1975 and an ugly dispute arose between them and the consultants and their respective organisations.

The Labour Party's policy is to eliminate private practice from the hospitals. The denial of facilities to surgeons to operate on private patients in public hospitals, the withdrawal of pathological and other services, the closing of clinics for private patients, the absence of private wards in those hospitals, would place every patient in the same position in regard to need for early treatment, the comfort and amenities he enjoys, and the interest and attention he receives from the medical and nursing staff. The public service, in short, is to be non-discriminatory so far as wealth or social position is concerned and only medical criteria will apply. Most of the arguments in support of this policy have turned on the allegations that the present practice enables well-off people to receive treatment sooner or at a more convenient time than other patients, that they have greater comfort and better food in the private wards, and that some consultants give priority to their private patients.

The policy adopted by the Labour Government is that while consultants may continue to give part-time service (that is, less than eleven sessions a week) to the National Health Service, private practice must be conducted entirely outside the state hospitals. Consultants giving less than the full number of sessions to the National Health Service would be discriminated against financially.

In considering this question, the long-term perspective is more important than the immediate results. Unlike the two systems of

public and private education, the health service has hitherto permitted a mixture of public and private treatment within a unified
framework. At present the health service hospitals are in general
much better equipped and staffed than most of the hospitals and
clinics outside. But if private patients were excluded from the
state hospitals, vast sums of money would soon be channelled into
the provision of hospitals available for such patients. Some of the
resources would no doubt come from the Middle East countries
whose rich patients fill many of the private beds in the leading
teaching hospitals, and American entrepreneurs are already
hovering over the British medical scene waiting for an opportunity
to exploit the wealthy patient. The relative quality of the public
and private sector hospitals might in those circumstances change
quite quickly. The rapid growth of BUPA and similar bodies
indicates the potential demand for private treatment. Above all,
it cannot be assumed that the most eminent physicians and
surgeons will always want to give at least part of their time, if
not all of it, to the National Health Service. The attractions of a
plush, highly paid private sector of medicine compared to a National
Health Service comprising only state patients and short of funds
might prove to be very persuasive. In any event we should have
two separate systems instead of one, with all the disadvantages
which exist in the field of education.

It is ironical that the egalitarian doctrine which is seeking to
integrate the public and independent systems of education should
simultaneously be trying to disintegrate the National Health Service.
Everyone should be aware of certain disadvantages in the present
system which could and should be removed; but the fundamental
question is whether the elimination of private wards and private
practice from the National Health Service will in the long run
have advantageous or detrimental effects on the leading hospitals
as centres of excellence. My own view is that the long-term results
may well prove to be detrimental.

One of the most divisive features of our society is the differences
of speech between people of different classes.[66] There is no other
country where this is so marked as in Britain, and its continued
existence is a formidable obstacle to social integration. It should
not be tolerated in a welfare society. What I am referring to has
no relation to regional differences of speech, which no one would
wish to abolish.

It cannot be seriously questioned that the welfare state has considerable achievements to its credit, though it still has a long way
to go. The question arises: What effect has this had on the outlook

of the nation? It is in a sense misleading to write or think of a national outlook, because people's views on most subjects vary greatly, as the public opinion polls show. Nevertheless, it is possible to observe certain trends in social psychology.

In spite of the many material improvements which have been made, public discontent appears to have increased. I do not recall any period during the past half-century in which so much criticism and dissatisfaction has been manifested about almost every aspect of life as is continually expressed at the present time, or so many demonstrations of protest against this, that and the other event or policy. Clamour, anger and discontent are the feelings most frequently expressed at public meetings, processions through the streets, and in the mass media. It is not easy to analyse the causes of this dissatisfaction: the loss of the Empire, the crumbling of the Commonwealth, our lack of political and military power, the weakness of our economy in comparison with other European countries and Japan, the disappearance of the special relationship with the US, may all have had an influence. What appears to be certain is that although resentment and anger may be caused by gross inequality, positive satisfaction has not resulted from the greater degree of equality and of equality of opportunity we have attained.

Dennis Gabor diagnoses the social discontent of contemporary society as existential nausea, which he asserts has always worried the rich, but which democracy has put within the reach of all. Some of the rich who were exceptionally gifted with will-power devoted their lives to the public good. But others, less favoured, took to alcoholism or crime in order to escape from boredom. Today, he observes, nausea, born of inner emptiness, is the cause of much juvenile delinquency and hooliganism.[67] Among the older age groups it leads to an obsession with bingo halls, slot machines and betting shops. This may be an exaggeration, but it contains an element of truth. A principal cause of dissatisfaction, of inner emptiness, of the desire to escape into some absorbing distraction, is the monotonous character of much routine work in industry, commerce and administration, though an increasing proportion is being taken over by computers and automation. 'Work', wrote Iris Murdoch, 'has become less unpleasant without becoming more significant. The gulf remains between the skilled and creative few and the unskilled and uncreative many.'[68]

To some extent the dissatisfaction which prevails in contemporary Britain may be due to the absence of a philosophy of the welfare state or any coherent ethical doctrine to support it.

What does the welfare state stand for? What are its basic aims? What does it require of us? No one has attempted to answer these questions.

We have a mixed economy of which by far the greater part is private enterprise. The left wing of the Labour Party, both inside and outside Parliament, and a number of trade union leaders, shop stewards and conveners, object to capitalism because it produces profits – when successful – and these are alleged to be the result of exploiting the workers, who are presumed to consist only of the wage-earners. The exponents of this view endeavour to cripple whole industries from functioning in a successful manner, and advocate their acquisition in whole or part by the state in order to safeguard the jobs which have sometimes been jeopardised by fiscal policies or industrial disruption. But when industries or firms are nationalised no change takes place in the attitude of the workpeople and their trade unions. They are still pursuing policies which will gain for themselves the maximum remuneration they can obtain as a result of their strategic position in the labour market, regardless of the effect on consumers, on other industries, on weaker groups of workers, on pensioners and others on fixed incomes, and on the economy as a whole. The acquisitive motive which Tawney denounced in capitalist society is reproduced unchanged among the workers in the publicly owned coal mines, railways, docks, and other public sector industries. It is here that we see the disastrous consequences of attempting to have a welfare state devoid of either a philosophy or an ethic.

Sir Frederick Catherwood sees the situation as one in which a third of the working population possesses the power to hold the other two-thirds to ransom. The power they wield is the power to take away, to force a company to face costs ten to twenty times as great as the wage claim, to impose a settlement which is borne by the other two-thirds of the working population without shop-floor power, such as the agricultural workers, those employed in distribution and the catering trades, those in small scattered workshops, garages, inshore fishermen, clerks and the like. The costs are also borne by the sick, the aged and the children. The result, in his view, is that everything is sacrificed to the preservation of the differentials of the higher-paid manual workers, as though they were the basic factor in our society.[69]

Many organisations could disrupt or destroy our society if they chose to follow the example of the militants in the docks, the railways, or the motorcar industry. The police, the fire service, the prison officers, are a few examples which spring to mind. They are restrained from doing so by a sense of responsibility which is based on the ethical principle that it is morally wrong to deprive society of an essential service in order to gain material benefit for oneself. Unless this principle can be accepted and extended by those who wield power on the shop floor in the highly organised, highly paid industries, in the schools, in the government departments, in the hospitals, in local government, and in other centres, it is difficult to see how the welfare state can develop into something better than we now have.

There are few systematic views about the nature and aims of the welfare state and scarcely any about the welfare society which is the *raison d'être* for its existence. The welfare state is not, as some people believe, just a collection of social services of a vaguely beneficial kind. Nor is it an instrument whose main purpose is to abolish poverty and assist the underprivileged or the handicapped, though it is deeply concerned about these and other categories in need. It is not a device for supporting or protecting the lazy, the workshy or the incompetent. And it is not committed to social and economic equality as the supreme good.

NOTES

1 August Heckscher, *The Public Happiness* (1963), pp. 203–4.
2 ibid.
3 ibid., p. 210.
4 ibid., pp. 212–13.
5 ibid., p. 209.
6 John S. Harris, *Government Patronage of the Arts in Great Britain* (1970), *passim*.
7 See pp. 57–8.
8 *Is Equality a Dream?* (1972), p. 6.
9 'Poverty as Relative Deprivation', in *Poverty, Inequality and Class Structure*, Dorothy Wedderburn (ed.) (1974), p. 15.
10 Thomas Wilson (ed.), *Pensions, Inflation and Growth* (1975), pp. 9–10.
11 'The Poor and the Poorest', in *Wealth, Income and Inequality*, A. B. Atkinson (ed.) (1973), pp. 365–6.
12 Robert Holman et al. *Socially Deprived Families in Britain* (1970), p. 160.
13 ibid., p. 144.
14 Social Security Statistics (HMSO, 1972), pp. 154–5.
15 Report of the Committee on One-Parent Families, Cmnd 5629 (HMSO, 1974), p. 5.
16 ibid., pp. 6, 490.
17 Report on Social Insurance and Allied Services, Cmnd 6404 (1972), para. 444, p. 165.
18 The figures are for November 1972. *Social Security Statistics 1972* (HMSO), table 34.99, p. 163.

19 Wilson, op. cit., pp. 364–5.
20 Frank Field, 'The New Poor: A Statistical Analysis' in *The New Poor*, Ian Henderson (ed.) (1973), pp. 57–9; *Circumstances of Families* Report (HMSO, 1967).
21 *Social Security Statistics 1972* (HMSO), table 34.95, p. 163.
22 Field, op. cit., pp. 63–4.
23 *Social Trends* (HMSO, 1973), table 49, p. 107.
24 Wilson, op. cit., pp. 11, 35, 361, 373.
25 ibid., p. 363.
26 ibid., pp. 343–5.
27 See, for example, J. C. Kincaid, *Poverty and Equality in Britain* (1973) Chapter 13; Ralph Miliband, 'Politics and Poverty' in Wedderburn (ed.), op. cit., Chapter 9.
28 Richard M. Titmuss, *Essays on the Welfare State* (1958), pp. 24–5.
29 ibid., pp. 24–5.
30 Peter Townsend and Nicholas Bosanquet (eds.), *Labour and Inequality* (1972), *passim.*
31 Kincaid, op. cit., pp. 246–7.
32 A. B. Atkinson, *Unequal Shares* (1972), *passim*; 'The Reform of Wealth in Britain' in *Taxation Policy*, Bernard Crick and William A. Robson (eds) (1973), pp. 100–1.
33 'Who's Rich?', *The Listener* (14 December 1972); Polanyi and Wood, How Much Inequality? (1974), *passim.*
34 Atkinson, op. cit., Part IV, pp. 251–2.
35 Cedric Sandford, 'Death Duties', in Crick and Robson (eds), op. cit., pp. 112–25.
36 Bertrand de Jouvenel 'Some Musings', in *Technology and Human Values* (1966), p. 33.
37 Piet Thoenes, *The Elite in the Welfare State* (1966), p. 149.
38 'The Improving Society' (fifth Reith Lecture), *The Listener* (12 December 1974), p. 760.
39 Enoch Powell, *The Welfare State* (1961), pp. 19–21.
40 Karl Mannheim, *Diagnosis of our Time* (1943), pp. 32–4.
41 Richard E. Caves and Associates (3rd imp. 1969), pp. 494–5.
42 See pp. 80–1.
43 The Dutch Provos comprised a miscellaneous group of young people rebelling against the commercialism, consumerism, computerisation and unquestioning acceptance of industrial society in the Netherlands. They attracted much attention and some public and press support in Amsterdam for a campaign directed against lack of play space for children, pollution, housing shortage, adulteration of food and the need for many social reforms. They presented a series of proposals for making Amsterdam more livable, known as the White Plans, and succeeded for a time in getting white bicycles provided free for use within the city. Other 'White Plans' dealt with air pollution, housing, the police, and road accidents. The Provo candidates ran for election to the municipal council in 1970 and won five of the forty-five seats. However, the movement petered out owing partly to the deviant behaviour of Provo councillors. They did succeed in focusing attention on widespread social and physical defects. Some of the Provos evolved a more ambitious scheme to establish a new Orange Free State in Europe with macro-biotic food grown and distributed on a non-

profit basis, freer education, and a ban on new industries. An excellent account of Provos is contained in *Delta*, a review of arts, life and thought in the Netherlands (Autumn 1967). See also *Holland Herald*, Vol. 5, No. 5, pp. 38–9.

44 Pauline Gregg, *The Welfare State* (1967), p. 110.

45 J. A. C. Brown, *The Social Psychology of Industry* (1970), p. 30.

46 The authoritarian is defined as a person who prefers to live in an ordered hierarchy of superiors on whom he can lean and of inferiors whom he can dominate. He can be contrasted with the humanist who, whatever his political beliefs or party affiliation, prefers to live in a society of mature and humanistic people. R. E. Money-Kyrle, *Psychoanalysis and Politics* (1951), p. 138.

47 Sir Geoffrey Vickers, 'Changing Ethics of Distribution', *Futures* (June 1971), p. 122.

48 I am indebted to Richard Batley and John Edwards, Research Fellows, Department of Sociology and Social Administration, University of Southampton, for supplying me with papers they have prepared containing much valuable information about the Urban Aid Programme. Their research was carried out for the Home Office.

49 The Local Government Grants (Social Need) Act 1969.

50 Cmnd 3703 (HMSO, 1968), para. 487.

51 For a reasoned criticism see David Donnison, 'Politics for Priority Areas', *Journal of Social Policy*, Vol. 3, no. 2, p. 127. Professor Donnison nonetheless advocates the continuation of these schemes.

52 *Social Trends* (HMSO, 1973), table 83, p. 134.

53 ibid., p. 135.

54 ibid., table 80, p. 131; table 91, p. 138.

55 Raphaella Bilski, 'Ideology and the Comprehensive Schools', *Political Quarterly*, Vol. 44 (April–June 1973), pp. 206, 208, 209, 210.

56 Public Schools Commission, First Report, Vol. 1 (HMSO, 1968), para. 6, p. 2.

57 *Children and their Primary Schools* (HMSO, 1967), Ch. 5 and pp. 464–5.

58 Public Schools Commission, First Report, Vol. 1, para. 9.

59 ibid, loc. cit.

60 ibid., paras 374–5.

61 ibid., para 394.

62 Public Schools Commission, Second Report, para. 117.

63 The Black Paper, edited by C. B. Cox and A. E. Dyson, was published by the Critical Quarterly Society, London, in 1969. For a good commentary see *The Times* (8 October 1969). See also Black Paper Two, especially the article on comprehensive disaster and the letter to Members of Parliament, pp. 6–8.

64 T. H. Marshall, *Sociology at the Crossroads* (1963), pp. 263–4.

65 See R. R. Pedley, 'Comprehensive Disaster', in *Fight for Education*, C. B. Cox and A. E. Dyson (eds) (1969), a Black Paper.

66 T. H. Pear, *English Social Differences* (1955), pp. 87–106.

67 Dennis Gabor, Professor of Electrical Engineering at Imperial College London, in *Technology and Human Values* (1966), p. 13.

68 Iris Murdoch, in Norman Mackenzie (ed.), *Conviction* (1958), p. 280.

69 A lecture on 'The Case for a Formal Grouping of Professional Institutions' at the Council of Science and Technological Institutes on 26 November 1974.

Chapter IX

Conclusions: Welfare State and Welfare Society

A theory of the welfare state should be based on the following propositions: the welfare state is devoted to the well-being of the whole society; it is as much concerned with maintaining or improving conditions for those who enjoy a good life style as with raising the standard of living of those who fall below an acceptable national minimum; it recognises no vested interests as standing in the way of maximising welfare, whether those of entrepreneurs, employees, distributors, consumers, landowners, developers, professionals, investors or financiers. Welfare is of unlimited scope. It extends to social and economic circumstances, conditions of work, remuneration, the character and scope of the social services, the quality of the environment, recreational facilities, and the cultivation of the arts. Among its essential elements are a high degree of personal freedom, including freedom of expression in speech and writing, freedom of movement, a political regime based on the principles of social democracy, and protection of individual citizens against abuse of power by public authorities and other organisations.

A welfare state requires the acceptance of legitimate authority, and obedience to the reign of law. It emphasises the duty of every man or woman to perform paid or voluntary work according to his or her capacity and ability. All sections of society must be willing to consider the rational justification for, and the adjustment of, the prevailing standards of remuneration and the existing distribution of wealth. Industrial disputes must be settled peaceably without disrupting the economy, either by negotiation or by an impartial tribunal.

The rights of citizens to the benefits of the welfare state must be accompanied by reciprocal duties. The need for complementary rights and obligations is particularly great in the fields of work, law and order, education, and the social services.

The environment is an essential aspect of welfare. Its improvement should be accorded a high priority in the allocation of resources both by public authorities and private undertakings. Individuals, companies or public authorities who degrade the environment by any form of pollution or disamenity should be held responsible by means of economic sanctions, or, where these are ineffective, by civil remedies or criminal penalties. Amenities should be protected by law.

The welfare state is committed to a continuous improvement of the social services in regard to their scope, adequacy and quality. It does not adhere to any general dogmas about means testing or consumer-charging, but applies whatever principle is likely to produce the most effective results in each service.

The standard of life in a welfare state is to be evaluated in terms of the quality of the environment, the benefits provided by the social services, the level of incomes and the distribution of wealth, job-satisfaction or dissatisfaction, leisure and recreation, health, education, housing, and similar criteria. The comprehensive concept of welfare will be rendered more intelligible by the quantification, where possible, of these components.

The existence of a sense of fellowship and public spirit throughout society is a basic need of the welfare state. This has special relevance in the spheres of race relations, sex discrimination, the settlement of industrial disputes, and relations within the place of employment.

Education and training policies should be designed and scrutinised for their effect on exceptionally gifted individuals as well as their impact on those of average ability.

A philosophy derived from these propositions may not add up to a prescription for Utopia; but if it were applied it would result in an immense increase of welfare for everyone. It would enhance the achievements, raise the standard of living, and improve the quality of life in our society to an incalculable degree.

Despite many unsolved problems of great difficulty and the rising level of conflict, the ethos of the welfare state places as much emphasis on full enjoyment as on full employment. 'In a way,' writes Professor Piet Thoenes of the Institute of Social Studies in The Hague, 'what makes the welfare state such a pleasant society is the stress on the good life. To earn a lot is, of course, still tremendously important, but there is a growing amount of "gardening" in daily life. "Gardening" here means focusing on personal things in your immediate surroundings. There is less interest for long-term, large-scale public affairs; more time for hobbies, collections, friendship and love.'[1] He thinks this attitude is in part a reaction to what is happening in the world around us. In that world there is more bureaucracy, more impersonal contacts, more organisation of every kind, both governmental and unofficial, more rationalisation in a society of ranks, certified qualifications, functions and administration.

There is little involvement in all this by the great majority of people, who feel they can do little to effect the course of events and think it best to leave public affairs to the Establishment. 'A logical consequence is widespread political apathy', writes this perceptive observer. Even in countries with less anomalous political parties than the Netherlands, political interest is ebbing. It is felt almost universally that politics are old-fashioned, a holdover from a generation that had not yet discovered that the real powers cannot be controlled by Parliament.[2] This state of mind is certainly as applicable to Britain as it is to the Netherlands.

It is an unhealthy state of mind, because it does not result from the apathy of contentment but from scepticism about politics, about the capacity of the governmental system and the ability of the political parties to cope with the problems of the day, and about the relevance of party politics to the things with which people are chiefly concerned.

The disassociation of the citizen from a lively interest in public affairs and from a sense of involvement in politics has been greatly influenced by the strong centralising trend which has occurred in recent decades. In the sphere of government this had led to the hegemony of the executive, the rise of the giant departments, nationalised industries operating on a scale of vast and unprecedented proportions, and a decline in the power and freedom of local authorities. In the economic sphere a similar trend can be detected in the mergers and take-overs of commercial firms resulting in the amalgamation of separate units into ever larger companies, with one board of directors replacing several; in multinational corporations whose activities cover more and more commodities in more and more countries; in trade unions, trade associations and professional bodies operating at the national or even international level rather than at the local level.

The welfare society should beware of the excessive concentration of power in the hands of the central government, public corporations and commercial undertakings, for they create a sense of impotence and remoteness in the minds of ordinary citizens which leads them to cease identifying with the course of public affairs because they feel unable to exercise any effective influence.

A perception of this growing indifference, scepticism and withdrawal underlies recent demands for, and promises of, 'participation', which has now become one of the in-words of current discussion. So far little progress has been made in explaining its meaning or showing how it could be a significant feature of the contemporary political and administrative scene. It would be inappropriate to explore the matter in detail here, and I am concerned only to stress its importance in the welfare state.

Centralisation has often been introduced in public administration by indignant politicians in order to remedy an alleged injustice resulting from the unequal provision of a service in different parts of the country. Despite the transfer of power, major differences usually continue to exist with little change. But the removal from a local community of the right to decide its own policies can lead to a loss of welfare.

Hitherto, the welfare state has been a centralising state, but this should not be regarded as a necessary or normal condition. Gunnar Myrdal rightly insists on 'the relevance of the Utopian, decentralised and democratic state where, within the bounds of ever more effective overall policies laid down for the whole national community, the citizens themselves carry more and more of the responsibility for organising their work and life by means of local and sectional cooperation and bargaining with only the necessary minimum of direct state interference.[3] This prescription accords fully with my own conviction and is both feasible and desirable.

Welfare resides not just in the output of government or the services which it delivers, but also in the processes by which government is carried on. Those who are most eager to reduce social and economic inequalities between classes and individuals are often those who are most anxious to concentrate power in the hands of ministers and the centralised bureaucracy, and thereby to increase the political and administrative inequality within the nation. This is not the way to build a welfare society. Welfare without freedom is as undesirable as freedom without welfare. The welfare state should embody the largest possible measure of both freedom and welfare. This can be achieved only if we have the insight to perceive that these are indissoluble links between these two basic elements of the good society. This applies to institutions no less than to individuals. Individual freedom is in such danger of erosion today in Britain that the time has come for a law embodying the fundamental civil rights of individuals to be enacted.

I have contended in this book that we cannot have a genuine

welfare state without a welfare society as its counterpart; that each is complementary to the other; and that so far we have achieved only a limited success in building a welfare state because there are so many elements in our society and our policies which are in conflict with that aim.

The changes which we need most at the present time to become a welfare society are as follows. First, everyone must understand and accept the duties that should complement the rights they enjoy in the welfare state. This applies particularly to the obligation to work, not to disrupt the economy, to maintain the basic public services and the nationalised industries, to make full use of publicly provided education, to respect the law and assist in maintaining order.

Second, every man (or woman) should try to ensure that those who speak for an organisation to which he belongs do represent his views; and if they do not, he should stand up and say so. In the trade unions and the student unions small bodies of militants, often elected by a tiny fraction of the members, are exercising vast powers or influence in the name of the whole organisation, although the great majority of the rank and file do not share their views and often disagree with them. The extent of this misrepresentation was revealed dramatically in the referendum on the Common Market, when a huge majority of the electors voted against the overwhelming opposition to Britain remaining in the EEC by the executive committees of the trade unions, the TUC, the National Executive Committee of the Labour Party and the Labour Party Annual Conference. The opportunity to disagree in a formal manner by a secret ballot seldom occurs, but the opportunity to protest, to reject or oppose extreme and disruptive proposals, to reveal the unrepresentative character of the so-called representatives, nearly always exists. It is seldom used by the silent majority owing to lack of courage and a mistaken sense of loyalty. A welfare society demands the moral courage to dissent in such circumstances.

Third, we must revise some of the traditional wisdom current in Britain. A cliché still in circulation is that in the Soviet Union and other communist countries in Eastern Europe the individual exists for the state while in Western civilisation the state exists for the individual. A more relevant question is whether non-governmental organisations of various kinds in this country exist for the benefit of the nation, or of the state, or of their members, or of themselves and those who manage them. This applies to some large commercial corporations, trade associations, trade unions, professional organisations, and even some charitable foundations. The answer is clear in the case of a body like the National Trust, which has served the interests of the nation in preserving our cultural heritage in a remarkable and unique way. Can one say as much of the National Council for Civil Liberties, or the Lord's Day Observance Society, or the trade unions whose restrictive policies cause so much overmanning in television production or the newspaper industry? Before the Second World War some leading political philosophers such as Harold Laski and G. D. H. Cole were pluralists because they feared and disliked the omnipotent state. Today, pluralism has taken over command of the economy and the social services, and threatens the authority of Parliament. The most effective restraint on the powers of the non-governmental bodies which have become centres of power must come from their own members.

Fourth, the stronger trade unions must understand that the unrestrained use of their powers to compel employers or the government to agree to inflationary wage settlements rather than face the disaster of a prolonged strike, are demonstrating the immorality of harnessing the ability to disrupt the economy to the cupidity and greed of an anti-social group of men. Left unchecked, such actions and attitudes will undermine the welfare state and render impossible the achievement of a welfare society. Such a society requires a limited use of power by whomsoever it is wielded; and restraint on its use must be exercised in the conscious knowledge that this is required in the interests of the larger community.

These prescriptions are not easy to carry out, but they are of fundamental importance. There is no short cut to the welfare society from the conflict, selfishness and lack of consensus which mark our present condition.

NOTES

1 'The Provos of Holland', *Delta* (Autumn 1967), p. 83.
2 ibid., p. 84.
3 *Beyond the Welfare State* (1960), p. 70.

ADDENDUM

After this book was written and ready for printing the Royal Commission on the Distribution of Income and Wealth published its first two reports. Report No. 1 deals with the estimated distribution of income and wealth among individuals. See *Ante*, p. 151.

Index